...OGY IN ACTION

HOW TO DO
SOCIAL RESEARCH

AUDREY DUNSMUIR

LYNN WILLIAMS

Collins Educational

An imprint of HarperCollins*Publishers*

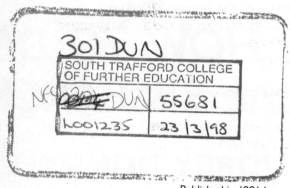
Published in 1991 by
CollinsEducational
An imprint of HarperCollins*Publishers*
77-85 Fulham Palace Road
Hammersmith
London W6 8JB

Reprinted 1992, 1993, 1994, 1996, 1997

First published 1990 by Unwin Hyman Ltd.
© Audrey Dunsmuir and Lynn Williams, 1990

British Library Cataloguing in Publication Data

Williams, Lynn
    How to do social research – (Sociology in action).
    I. Sociology. Research. Methodology
    I. Title   II. Dunsmuir, Audrey   III. Series
    301.092

ISBN 0–00–322242–X

Cover by Oxford Illustrators
Designed by Bob Wright

Typeset by Dorchester Typesetting Group Ltd.
Printed in Great Britain by
Scotprint Ltd., Musselburgh.

Contents

Section 3   Skills for a Sociology Course

General Bibliography

Index

Acknowledgements

Introduction

The aim of this book is to help students become practising sociologists. They need to understand how research has been done by other sociologists, be able to evaluate that research and to carry out a personal sociological enquiry using different research methods. The book aims to equip them with the necessary skills to cope with the different elements of assessment at A-level and A/S-level, and with basic skills of note-taking and revision.

With these aims in mind, **Section 1** provides, through examples, a good basic grounding in methodology. What are the different methods used by sociologists? What are their relative strengths and weaknesses? In what circumstances are different methods appropriate? The emphasis throughout this section is on encouraging students to ask questions about research and to judge its usefulness for themselves. It is felt that students need to be able to evaluate published research examples constructively before they are able to conduct their own research. There is no attempt to discuss broader theoretical considerations, although these issues are central to a discussion of methodology and it is assumed that the student has some background theoretical knowledge.

Section 2 builds upon the understanding developed by **Section 1** and guides students through ways in which they themselves can practise sociology. By providing worked examples of manageable pieces of research, students are given practice in the skills needed for carrying out their own research.

Section 3 concentrates more explicitly on the demands of examination assessment at A-level and A/S-level. Guidance, activities and examples are provided to help students master the skills of reading and note-taking, essay writing and answering stimulus-response questions and preparing for the final examination.

It is envisaged that the book will be *used* by students rather than just read chronologically. It may be that some sections are more useful than others at different stages of their course. Doing sociology may often be uncomfortable, causing students to question their own values, but we believe that more than any other subject it provides an opportunity to contribute actively to an understanding of reality.

Audrey Dunsmuir
Lynn Williams

Introduction

Sociologists enquiring into a topic have the choice of a wide range of different methods of research. They may carry out their research using *secondary data*, that is, re-analysing data which already exists such as statistics, newspaper reports, diaries and historical documents. Alternatively, they may conduct their own *primary research*, for example using a social survey, different types of interview or participant observation. Another way in which methods may be classified is in terms of whether they are *quantitative* or *qualitative*. Quantitative research aims to collect facts and figures using methods like the social survey or analysis of statistics. Qualitative research aims to gain a more in-depth understanding of a situation; this may involve informal interviews, participant observation or analysis of personal diaries or autobiographies, for example.

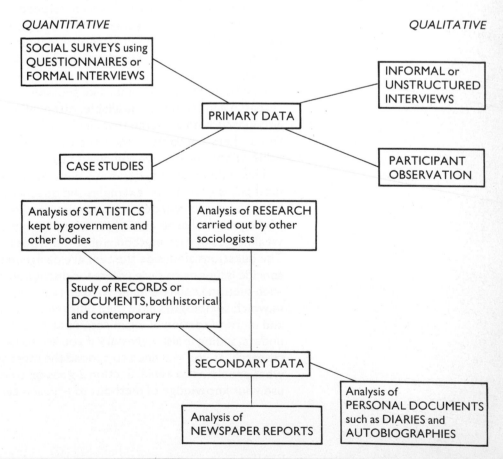

QUANTITATIVE *QUALITATIVE*

SOCIAL SURVEYS using QUESTIONNAIRES or FORMAL INTERVIEWS

INFORMAL or UNSTRUCTURED INTERVIEWS

PRIMARY DATA

CASE STUDIES

PARTICIPANT OBSERVATION

Analysis of STATISTICS kept by government and other bodies

Analysis of RESEARCH carried out by other sociologists

Study of RECORDS or DOCUMENTS, both historical and contemporary

SECONDARY DATA

Analysis of NEWSPAPER REPORTS

Analysis of PERSONAL DOCUMENTS such as DIARIES and AUTOBIOGRAPHIES

The actual methods chosen by a sociologist depend on a variety of factors. It is sometimes argued that the main factor determining choice of method is theoretical perspective. A full account of the different perspectives in sociology can be found in any major textbook. The different perspectives can be divided into two basic schools of thought, *positivists* and *interpretivists*. Positivists believe that it is possible to study the world in the same way as the natural world. They aim to produce 'social facts' or broad generalisations about human behaviour. The sociologist is regarded as the neutral collector of facts; he/she is able to gain objectivity by standing back from his/her own values. By following their methods, positivists hope to achieve a 'scientific' study of society. Therefore, it is commonly argued that positivists will use quantitative (statistical) techniques of data collection since these are felt to be more reliable and can be easily checked or verified by another sociologist conducting the same research.

Conversely, interpretivists believe that the social world is different from the natural world, both because the subject matter (people) is unpredictable – people attach meaning to their behaviour and do not always respond to stimuli in patterned ways – and because sociologists themselves are part of the world they are studying and cannot be totally objective. Interpretivists therefore argue that social facts are no more than social constructs and that sociology should aim at a more in-depth understanding of human behaviour. As a result, it is commonly argued that they will use more qualitative techniques since these allow the researcher to understand the meaning which people attach to their behaviour.

In practice, this link between theory and method is far too simplistic. A great deal of research is carried out without *any* guiding perspective. In some cases the subject itself will dictate the most appropriate methods. Much sociological research is commissioned by public bodies, who themselves dictate what sort of data they want to be produced; in these cases the sociologist has little choice of what method to use. Sociologists might also be influenced by the attitudes of their colleagues or by what is regarded as 'good' research at a particular point in time.

Finally, practical restraints, like the time available to complete the research and the finance available, often influence the method chosen. It is also inaccurate to assume that all research uses only one method. Many researchers aim to study their topic in a variety of ways recognising the value of both qualitative and quantitative data.

This section looks in detail at a number of studies using the main research methods outlined. The examples and questions which go with them have been chosen to help develop an understanding of the methods themselves – of the practical problems which might be experienced, of the strengths and weaknesses of each method and of the types of data which are produced. The questions alongside the text are designed to make you think about specific issues or to raise points for discussion, whereas those at the end of each section require a fuller written response. An understanding of the way in which sociologists have used different methods is essential for the theory and method section of examinations at A-level and A/S-level. This understanding is also necessary if you are to carry out your own sociological research, as you will need to choose the most suitable method and know what problems to avoid. Section 2 goes on to look at ways in which you can use your knowledge of methods to plan and carry out your own research.

Method A: Observation

Observation involves a researcher gaining membership or attachment to a group, so he/she can study social action in its natural context, undisturbed, as it occurs. This could mean joining a group of mental patients in a hospital, accompanying a teenage gang to clubs/cafés or observing student/teacher behaviour in the classroom.

Observation attempts to achieve a detailed picture of social reality as experienced by the actors. The aim is to see the world through the eyes of those you are studying. How do they make sense of the hospital environment, the fight on Friday night, or being told off by the teacher? The researcher must strive to acquire an understanding of social action without imposing his/her own definitions and values.

A researcher using this method must decide if he/she will adopt an approach which is either:

- **covert** – the subjects will be unaware of the researcher's true identity and purpose. This often entails the researcher assuming a false identity, e.g. James Patrick in *A Glasgow Gang Observed* identified himself to the gang as Tim's 'haufer' i.e. 'best friend', or;

- **overt** – the researcher will disclose him/herself but sometimes disguise the true nature of research. For example, Gans's study *The Levitowners* attempted to investigate the impact of new town life. He presented the purpose of his research to the people of Levitown as a study on the community from a historical perspective.

The examples included in this chapter, *A Glasgow Gang Observed* by J. Patrick, and *Tearoom Trade* by L. Humphreys, use covert participant observation to study 'deviant groups' to which they might otherwise be denied access. Humphreys' research shows how participant observation can be made more systematic and as a result more objective by use of an observation schedule. Patrick's observation is less structured and more impressionistic, but gives a clear idea of the type of data which participant observation can yield. The example of research by Eileen Barker on page 59 uses overt observation next to other methods of research and clearly shows the relative advantages and disadvantages of overt rather than covert observation. All three studies illustrate the problems a participant observer has in adopting a role as well as identifying the strengths and weaknesses of this method of research.

James Patrick: *A Glasgow Gang Observed*

James Patrick was a teacher at an approved school in Scotland. He took up th
invitation by Tim – a sixteen-year-old juvenile offender – to come and see fo
himself 'whit the score wis' in the 'Young team' (a Glasgow street gang of
which Tim was leader).

Patrick, posing as Tim's friend from the approved school, took up this
challenge. Having been briefed by Tim on the appropriate style of dress and
considering himself aware of the local dialect and slang (an assumption which
was to prove his first mistake), Patrick met and joined the gang.

Patrick argues that his work offers a descriptive account of life in a gang,
which he met on twelve occasions between October 1966 and January 1967.
He writes:

> In all I spent just under 120 hours in the field; and as my involvement with the
> gang deepened, so the hours lengthened until towards the end of January I was ir
> the company of the gang during one weekend from seven o'clock on Friday
> evening until six on Sunday morning.
>
> I have deliberately allowed some years to pass between the completion of the
> fieldwork and publication. The main reasons for the delay have been my interest
> in self-preservation, my desire to protect the members of the gang, and my fear
> of exacerbating the gang situation in Glasgow which was receiving nationwide
> attention in 1968 and 1969. Reasons of personal safety also dictate the use of a
> pseudonym.
>
> What follows is not a study of Glasgow, or of Glasgow youth in general, or of a
> particular community within the city. It is a small-scale piece of research which is
> in no way a statistical survey and so the conclusions may well be of a restricted
> character.

How does this make his work restricted and unrepresentative?

Before meeting the gang Patrick had to prepare for making an entry.

> I began to concentrate on making my physical appearance acceptable to the
> group. I was prepared to give my age as seventeen, although this point was never
> questioned. In fact I was able to pass myself off as a mate of a fifteen-year-old
> boy; my exact age remained indeterminate but apparently acceptable. Clothes
> were another major difficulty. I was already aware of the importance attached to
> them by gang members in the school and so, after discussion with Tim, I bought
> the suit I have described in the first paragraph. Even here I made two mistakes.
> Firstly, I bought the suit outright with cash instead of paying it up, thus attracting
> both attention to myself in the shop and disbelief in the gang when I innocently
> mentioned the fact. Secondly, during my first night out with the gang, I fastened
> the middle button of my jacket as I am accustomed to do. Tim was quick to spot
> the mistake. The boys in the gang fastened only the top button; with this
> arrangement they can stand with their hands in their trouser pockets and their
> jackets buttoned.

What might have happened if Patrick had not paid attention to these points?

Once he was accepted into the gang, Patrick began recording his
observations; and these make illuminating reading about life in a gang. Here
are some examples of the types of incidents he records.

Saturday afternoon

> Tim began walking, with the others trailing behind him. We had been walking for
> some time, 'jist dossin'', when Tim had an idea. 'Let's get right intae that Lib'ry',
> he said, pointing to one of Glasgow's Public Libraries.
>
> Running into the building, we ignored the Lending Section because of its
> turnstile, and burst into the Reading Room. Dan McDade and Billy Morton began
> setting fire to the newspapers on display, as Tim and the others pushed books off

tables and emptied shelves of encyclopedias and reference books. I 'kept the edge up' at the outer door and shouted 'Polis!' as soon as I dared. Dave Malloy was trying to set alight the newspapers being read by old-age pensioners or down-and-outs. One old man beside the door, wearing woollen gloves with the finger pieces cut out, was reading with his face screwed up against the print which he deciphered with the aid of a magnifying glass. Jimmy Barrow's last act was to knock this glass from his hand as he ran past. En route to the street, a male attendant in a green uniform was punched and kicked out of the way. Some, behind me, could hardly run for laughing.

What do these extracts tell us about life in the gang?

Weapons

The Malloys* boasted of being able to outwit any policeman who searched them; Tim, for instance, claimed to have been 'raked' one night while 'kerryin'' and to have escaped arrest for possessing an offensive weapon. The trick he had picked up from his elder brothers, none of whom had ever been caught in possession. Before leaving the house, John used to tie a short blade to his wrist with a piece of string; he then concealed it by rolling down his shirt sleeve over the knife which rested alongside his forearm. Tim adopted the same technique, but in addition, was fond of carrying his favourite weapon – an open, lock-back razor. Harry Johnstone thought this 'sleekit'. At nights when they met, Harry would ask Tim, 'Are ye kerryin'?' 'Me kerryin'? Are ye kiddin'?' Yet in a fight, I was told, 'a wee blade comes oot oan the sleekit – a wee loak-back or somethin'.'

* two brothers

Rivalry between gangs

Both sides now wanted a showdown. Tim's 'goin' oan the creep' was considered by some of the more peripheral members of the Young Team as despicable as 'chibbin' lassies', but they were circumspect in not voicing their opinions too loudly. The only solution, Tim thought, was 'tae battle it oot.' During Christmas week, the gang talk became more frenzied. The pros and cons of various battlefields were discussed. It was up to the Barnes Road* to make the first move. 'They says they're comin' up tae oor pitch, bu' they're aye sayin' it an' they never dae.' In this climate of mounting excitement every boy in the area within the aegis of the Fleet and all other associated gangs had been alerted and told to be armed. As one of their number, I was handed a hatchet.

My reluctance to carry weapons, noticed earlier, now aroused hostility. The situation had not been helped by may 'takin' a back seat durin' the action'. Dave Malloy was my principal accuser; whenever the conversation allowed it, he never failed to make a jeering remark at my expense. The sneering had turned to pushing and jostling and a 'square-go' between us was on the cards. Without Tim's constant interventions on my behalf I would have been unable to sustain my role.

What dilemmas did Patrick face as a result of being a covert observer?

Are these dilemmas inevitable with covert observation?

* a rival gang

The party

At the party in January, Tim was presented with twenty-odd pills and took four right away. A few of these half-red, half-black pellets were pressed upon me and I was invited to sample these 'Black Bombers'. Putting two in my mouth I stuck them to the inside of my cheek and drank deeply from a can of lager. Only one of the pills stayed in place and I spat it out at the first available opportunity. But by then only the capsule was left and the white powder covered my tongue.

This experience provided me with the opening I needed and for once Tim spoke at length on the subject. After 'bein' in the clouds', he dreaded 'the horrors' of the following morning. 'Ye imagine every-thin' yir afrighted fur. Chibbin' some-wan tae death in the street wi' everyboady at the windaes watchin' who's dain' it – and the polis chasin' ye, and you runnin' fur miles an' miles.'

Patrick relies on his memory to record his observations. What problems does this present?

Laud Humphreys: *Tearoom Trade*

Tearoom Trade is a study of homosexual activity in men's public toilets in America. The aim of the research is:

> . . . to describe for the reader the social structure of impersonal sex, the mechanisms that make it possible. How then, does such an operation work? What rules govern it? What roles may people play in it? What sort of ritual sustains the action? What are the risks – to players and others – of such activity? What kinds of people find the tearooms inviting for sexual experience and how do they relate this behaviour to the rest of their lives?

Humphreys' study included ethnographic research or participant observation, and both informal and formal interviews.

The observation

The ethnographic research, which lasted for two years, fell into two stages. In the initial period Humphreys observed in an unsystematic way. At this stage he made research notes into a tape recorder in his car as soon as possible after each observation. Having gained a better understanding of the culture he was studying Humphreys was able to 'tighten up' his research. The second stage was, therefore, more systematic observation. A detailed 'systematic observation sheet' was filled out for fifty homosexual encounters observed by Humphreys and for a further thirty encounters observed by a 'co-operating participant'. He recorded the different people present and their position in the room, the age, clothes, etc. of the participants and other factors like the time of day. The sheet was filled out immediately after the event with more detailed comments added later.

What are the problems with recording observation after an event? Do you feel that using a systematic observation sheet reduces these problems?

Interviews

Two types of interviews were used to supplement the data gained from participant observation. Humphreys developed a verbal relationship with twelve of the participants and informed them of the nature of his research. They agreed to be interviewed and some of the interviews were taped. These interviews could not be regarded as in any way representative but were useful to Humphreys as a way of checking that his observations were valid.

A further fifty formal interviews were completed with men who Humphreys had observed in homosexual encounters. He gained this sample by noting car registration numbers parked by participants in tearooms and tracking down the names and addresses of their owners. He then arranged for one hundred such men to be included in a survey which he was conducting on the social health of men in the community. These men had no knowledge of why they had been included in the survey. After the survey was completed Humphreys took out the results for his 'deviant sample'. For various reasons he received only fifty completed surveys. Information from these questionnaires was used to discover basic demographic information – such as age, marital status etc. – about his sample of homosexuals. He took great care to protect the identity of his respondents.

What ethical problems does this present?

Problems with covert observation

Humphreys identifies three main problems associated with covert participant observation, as follows:

1. The problem of becoming a 'natural part of the life of the observed':

> I had to enter the subculture as would any newcomer and to make contact with respondents under the guise of being another gay guy.
>   Such entry is not difficult to accomplish. Almost any taxi driver can tell a customer where to find a gay bar. A guide to such gathering places may be purchased for five dollars. The real problem is not one of making contact with the subculture but of making the contact 'stick'. Acceptance does not come easy, and it is extremely difficult to move beyond superficial contact in public places to acceptance by the group and invitations to private and semiprivate parties.

Why is it important to be totally accepted?

In his observation in the tearooms he usually adopted the role of the voyeur-lookout. A voyeur is someone who gains satisfaction from observing the activity of other people without actively taking part. He argues:

> By serving as a voyeur-lookout, I was able to move around the room at will, from window to window, and to observe all that went on without alarming my respondents or otherwise disturbing the action. I found this role much more amenable and profitable than the limited roles assumed in the earlier stages of research. Not only has being a watchqueen enabled me to gather data on the behavioral patterns, it has facilitated the linking of participants in homosexual acts with particular automobiles.

What ethical problems are presented by Humphreys adopting this role?

2. The problem of maintaining scientific integrity, that is, taking a value-free approach to the research:

> My first concern has been for objective validity – to avoid distortion of the data either by my presence or my presuppositions. I have also desired to make future replications and comparative studies possible, by being as systematic as possible in recording and gathering data.

He used two techniques to achieve this aim:

i)

> I want to describe the techniques employed in 'tightening up' my data. Following the preliminary observations, I developed a 'Systematic Observation Sheet' on which to record my observations. This form – used by myself in describing fifty encounters and by a cooperating participant in the recording of thirty others – helped to assure consistent and thorough recording of the observed encounters.

ii)

> It has been my practice throughout the analysis of the research data to discuss developing concepts and theories with cooperating respondents. (I consider this sort of inside evaluation one of the more valuable means of validation.)

What is the value of this?

3. 'The problems of ethical integrity' – do sociologists have the right to observe people's private behaviour without revealing their role?:

> Are there, perhaps, some areas of human behavior that are not fit for social scientific study at all? Should sex, religion, suicide, or other socially sensitive concerns be omitted from the catalogue of possible fields of sociological research?

Humphreys argues

> I believe that preventing harm to his respondents should be the *primary* interest of the scientist. We are not, however, protecting a harrassed population of deviants by refusing to look at them.

Humphreys discusses ethics with regard to his study at great length. His arguments have been reproduced in detail here because they raise a number of important issues. He identifies four ethical issues which are important for all sociological research, not just covert participant observation.

Situation ethics

> Let it be noted that any conceivable method employable in the study of human behavior has at least some potential for harming others. Even the antiseptic strategies involved in studying public archives may harm others if they distort, rather than contribute to, the understanding of social behavior. Criminologists may study arrest statistics, as filtered to us through the FBI, without stirring from the safety of their study chairs, but such research methods may result in the creation of a fictitious 'crime wave,' a tide of public reaction, and the eventual production of a police state – all because the methods may distort reality.
>
> There are no 'good' or 'bad' methods – only 'better' or 'worse' ones. Neither interview schedules nor laboratory experiments nor participant observation can be neatly classified as involving either 'open' or 'disguised' approaches. I have never known an interviewer to be completely honest with his respondents; were this so, the whole concern with constructing an 'effective' questionnaire could be dropped. Neither does any researcher ever have adequate insight for a perfect representation of his identity; it is always a matter of greater or lesser misrepresentation. . . .
>
> . . . The researcher must also keep in mind that no method can ever be completely safe for himself or his respondents, and thus must weigh it in relation to others that may be applied in any instance. The ethics of social science are situation ethics.

■ **Why might research based on crime statistics be regarded as unethical? Do you accept this?**

Problems of misrepresentation

It has been argued that it is unethical for a sociologist to deliberately misrepresent his or her identity or the aims of the research in order to gain information. There are two ways in which Humphreys may be criticised for misrepresentation.

Firstly, in his role as observer in the tearooms, he argues that:

> Since one's identity within the interaction membrane of the tearoom is represented only in terms of the participant role he assumes, there was no misrepresentation of my part as an observer: I was indeed a 'voyeur,' though in the sociological and not the sexual sense. My role was primarily that of watchqueen, and that role I played well and faithfully. In that setting, then, I misrepresented my identity no more than anyone else. Furthermore, my activities were intended to gain entrance not to 'a private domain' but to a public restroom. The only sign on its door said 'Men', which makes me quite eligible for entering.

Secondly, he says that:

> . . . I interviewed persons I had observed in the tearooms under the pretext of a social health survey. Here it should be noted that all interviews were in fact made as part of a larger social health survey, and abstracted data from my interviews are already in use in that study. The problem then may be viewed in two ways: first, I gave less than full representation of what I was doing, though

without giving false representation. I wore only one of two possible hats, rather than going in disguise. Second, I made multiple use of my data. Is it unethical to use data that someone has gathered for purposes one of which is unknown to the respondent? With the employment of proper security precautions, I think such multiple use is quite ethical; it is frequently employed by anyone using such data banks as the records of the Bureau of Census.

Do you find these arguments convincing?

Problems of confidentiality

Humphreys made every possible effort in his research to protect the identity of the people he was studying.

Problems of consequentiality

It is important that sociological research should not give rise to negative consequences for any of those being studied.

He argues that his research however would be more likely to reduce stereotypes and negative reactions to homosexual activity in tearooms than to increase public and legal reaction.

Humphreys argues that research is unethical if:

> (i) **The sociologist misrepresents his or her identity or aims to gain information**
> (ii) **The sociologist breaks confidence**
> (iii) **The research has negative consequences for the people being studied.**

To what extent do you accept his arguments that his research is not unethical?

Why use participant observation?

Humphreys outlines several reasons for using participant observation, and covert observation in preference to overt observation:

> I employed the methods described herein not because they are the most accurate in the sense of 'neatness' or 'cleanness' but because they promised the greatest accuracy in terms of faithfulness to people and actions as they live and happen. These are strategies that I judged to be the least obtrusive measures available – the least likely to distort the real world. . . .
>
> In the first place, I am convinced that there is only *one* way to watch highly discreditable behavior and that is to pretend to be in the same boat with those engaging in it. To wear a button that says 'I Am a Watchbird, Watching You' into a tearoom, would instantly eliminate all action except the flushing of toilets and the exiting of all present. . . .
>
> The second reason is to prevent distortion. Hypothetically, let us assume that a few men could be found to continue their sexual activity while under observation. How 'normal' could that activity be? How could the researcher separate the 'show' and the 'cover' from standard procedures of the encounter? A stage is a suitable research site only for those who wish to study the 'onstage' behavior of actors. . . .
>
> My concern in this study has been with the description of a specific style of deviant behavior and of the population who engage in that activity. Beyond such systematic, descriptive analyses, I have tried to offer, in the light of deviance theory, some explanation as to why and how these people participate in the

particular form of behavior described. I have not attempted to test any pre-stated hypotheses. Such an approach tends to limit sociological research to the imagery of the physical sciences. It seems to me equally valid to apply a number of measures to one population or one type of social interaction for the purpose of describing that encounter and its participants. . . .

Hypotheses should develop *out of* such ethnographic work, rather than provide restrictions and distortions from its inception.

■ What theoretical perspective has guided Humphreys' research? How has it influenced his method?

Findings

Through his research Humphreys questions stereotyped ideas about homosexual activities in public toilets. Firstly, he argues that the men involved are very ordinary; that they do not fit any particular 'type' but come from all walks of life including middle-class professionals. Many of the men were married and several of them had children. Secondly, he suggests that public concern that unsuspecting men, especially youths, may be drawn into homosexual activity is unfounded. The encounters in the tearooms followed a set ritual and 'straight' people not giving definite signals were never approached. Humphreys suggests that the greatest threat to society is provided by police action in disclosing the homosexual activity with the consequent disruption of family life. He recommends that as tearoom activities do not damage society police surveillance should be relaxed.

■ QUESTIONS

1. **A covert observer must learn his/her role so well that he/she fits completely into the group. Identify what this involved for both Humphreys and Patrick.**

2. **To what extent did Patrick's and Humphreys' presence influence or shape the events they were observing? Give examples.**

3. **Patrick and Humphreys relied on two very different methods of recording their data. Briefly describe them and comment on their effectiveness.**

4. **What ethical problems are presented by the use of covert observation? Use examples from both pieces of research.**

5. **Humphreys argues that all methods of research may present ethical problems. Explain this and say to what extent you agree, using examples to illustrate your answer.**

6. **What are the strengths of covert participant observation for studying deviant behaviour? What disadvantages or problems might other more direct methods have?**

7. **Some critics would argue that participant observation is too impressionistic and unscientific. Why might they argue this? How would its supporters defend it against this claim? Illustrate your answer with examples.**

Read the section on pages 59-63 before answering these questions:

8. **Eileen Barker chooses to study the Moonies by 'being an outsider on the inside'. What advantages does this role of overt participation observation give her?**

9. **Using all three studies, draw up a table to show the relative advantages and disadvantages of both overt and covert participant observation.**

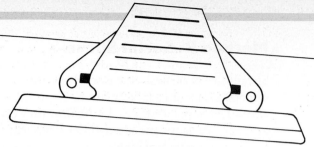

Checklist

ADVANTAGES

1. Social behaviour is in its natural setting, undisturbed.

2. Offers an opportunity for small scale, detailed research.

3. Gives validity to the meanings actors attach to their action.

4. Constructs the world according to the actors' values/norms and language.

5. It may sometimes be used, before carrying out a survey, in order to discover what questions are relevant to ask.

DISADVANTAGES

1. The researcher may become too involved and therefore be a poor observer.

2. How representative is the study group? Are generalisations possible?

3. How do you record information accurately without bias? Often it is impossible to use a tape recorder or to take notes, therefore the researcher must rely on memory.

4. Is it morally/ethically acceptable?

5. It may be physically dangerous for the observer.

6. It may take a long time to get in, stay in, get out.

7. Is it really possible for a researcher to lose his/her own values and study a group objectively?

8. The observer's presence may change or influence the behaviour of the group.

■ **PROJECT**

1. **Select three questions on Education (pages 68-69) that lend themselves to the observation method of enquiry. Consider whether covert or overt observation is most suitable.**

2. **Attempt your own covert observation with a group you already belong to, e.g. your family, your peer group, a sports club. Keep a diary to record events and any problems which you experience.**

Method B: Social Surveys

Social surveys are carried out when a researcher wishes to gain statistical information from a large number of people, usually to make generalisations about the population as a whole. Because they are large scale with an emphasis on facts, social surveys usually ask closed questions (with a limited number of responses) which are pre-coded to allow analysis on a computer. Questions are standardised, in that everyone is asked the same questions in the same order, and it is therefore assumed that people's responses are comparable since they are responding to exactly the same question. Occasionally there are also some open or free choice questions. Question wording in surveys is very important since the quality of results is inevitably affected by the questions. If respondents do not understand the words used or if their preferred response just is not there the survey cannot produce useful results. It is for this and other reasons that most surveys are preceded by a pilot survey which aims to discover and rectify any problems before the actual survey is carried out; this can also give the researcher some idea of the amount of time that the interview or questionnaire will take and the best order in which to ask the questions.

Since the aim of a survey is to make general statements it is important that it is answered by a group of people who are representative of the population being studied and not by a group which is biased in some way. Since it is too costly and time consuming to survey everyone who is relevant to a study, a sample is usually taken and the extent to which the sample is truly random (everyone having an equal chance of being included) is crucial to the reliability of the study. To achieve a representative sample a researcher must not only select by random techniques but must also ensure a high response rate to the survey.

Social surveys may be sent by post in the form of a questionnaire, they may be given to groups of people as in a school or a factory, or they may be carried out by an interviewer reading out the questions and recording the answers. Each particular method has its own strengths and weaknesses. The two examples of social surveys which follow both use a structured interview to ask their questions but are quite different in other ways. Townsend's research is more comprehensive, aiming to make generalisations to the population as a whole, whereas Willmott's research is smaller scale and largely exploratory. Both illustrate clearly the stages necessary in conducting a social survey and indicate some of the strengths and weaknesses of this approach.

Peter Townsend: *Poverty in the United Kingdom*

This is a large scale social survey with two main aims:

> Our first practical object was to estimate the numbers in the population at different levels of living, particularly the numbers living in poverty or on the margins of poverty. Our second was to find what are the characteristics and problems of those in poverty and thus contribute to the development of an explanation for poverty.

Although the book was published in 1979 the fieldwork began in 1965 and was completed in 1969. The intervening ten years were taken up analysing the mass of statistics produced. There were four stages to the research:

1. Pilot research into certain minority groups.
2. Preparatory and pilot work on the main survey.
3. The main survey.
4. Follow-up surveys in poor areas of four parliamentary constituencies.

Why do you think analysis took so long? What problem does this give rise to?

The pilot research conducted between 1965 and 1968 had several uses.

> The pilot research which was carried out between 1965 and 1968 helped to sharpen methods of measuring unemployment and sub-employment, disability and sickness, and styles of living, including amenities at home and in the locality. During the autumn of 1967 a questionnaire running to 120 pages, which was planned for the main survey, was applied to 150 households scattered in and around London . . .
>   Our own pilot work and other research studies have shown that families living on low incomes are far less homogeneous than has been supposed hitherto. Fatherless families, families dependent on low earnings, families with a chronically sick or disabled adult and families with an unemployed head have problems which are very different from each other as well as those which are common. Even within these groups there are big differences, as between widows and separated wives within the category of fatherless families, for example.

What did Townsend learn from conducting a pilot survey?

The main survey was carried out in 1968-9 in 51 constituencies in the United Kingdom. A total of 2052 households covering 6098 individuals were involved. At the same time, four parallel local surveys were carried out in poor areas covering 1208 households or 3950 individuals.

Before the research could be conducted it was necessary to devise ways of measuring poverty. Townsend identified three possible measures of poverty:

Definitions of Poverty

1. Comparisons with supplementary benefit levels as used by the government in its own survey.
2. Comparisons with average levels of living (median, for example, and mean income of different types of household and mean disposable personal income).
3. An attempt to identify deprivation on the basis of inability to participate in even a substantial number of activities and customs followed by the majority of the population of the United Kingdom.

Townsend's preferred measure was the third. He believed that it was possible to devise an 'objective measure of relative poverty' that we could establish for different household-types the level of income below which they were unable to adopt a style of life which was generally expected in our society. He called this measure the 'deprivation index'. He devised sixty indices of deprivation including all areas of personal, household and social life. A summary index is shown below with the percentage of the population who were deprived on each measure:

The deprivation index

Characteristic	% of population
1. Has not had a week's holiday away from home in last 12 months	53.6
2. *Adults only*. Has not had a relative or friend to the home for a meal or snack in the last 4 weeks	33.4
3. *Adults only*. Has not been out in the last 4 weeks to a relative or friend for a meal or snack	45.1
4. *Children only* (under 15). Has not had a friend to play or to tea in the last 4 weeks	36.3
5. *Children only*. Did not have party on last birthday	56.6
6. Has not had an afternoon or evening out for entertainment in the last two weeks	47.0
7. Does not have fresh meat (including meals out) as many as four days a week	19.3
8. Has gone through one or more days in the past fortnight without a cooked meal	7.0
9. Has not had a cooked breakfast most days of the week	67.3
10. Household does not have a refrigerator	45.1
11. Household does not usually have a Sunday joint (3 in 4 times)	25.9
12. Household does not have sole use of four amenities indoors (flush WC; sink or washbasin and cold-water tap; fixed bath or shower; and gas or electric cooker)	21.4

Do you agree that these are indices of deprivation? Working with a friend, draw up your own list of things which you think could be used to measure deprivation today. Use your list to measure the level of deprivation experienced by a sample of people.

To establish his poverty line, Townsend plotted graphs showing the number of deprivations suffered at different income levels. He found an income level – obviously varying it according to family size – below which the number of deprivations suffered increased disproportionately. He took this level of income as his poverty line.

It is important to recognise that Townsend accepted that because of the variety of individual/cultural or religious preferences different people would suffer some of these deprivations. The crucial point in measuring poverty was the *total* number of deprivations experienced.

Different items in the index reflect the fact that some customs or activities are common to the household, but others apply only to individuals within the household. No single item by itself, or pair of items by themselves, can be regarded as symptomatic of general deprivation. People are idiosyncratic and will indulge in certain luxuries and apply certain prohibitions, for religious, moral, educational and other reasons, whether they are rich or poor. Families in certain situations are not necessarily deprived if they do not have a week's holiday; or if they do not have an afternoon or evening outside the home; or if they do not have a Sunday joint, because they may have other compensating activities or customs. This is why deprivation is difficult at the margins to detect. A score of 5 or 6 or more is regarded as highly suggestive of deprivation. Twenty per cent of households scored an average of 6 or more.

What do we mean by an 'objective measure of relative poverty'?

Do you agree that Townsend's measure is 'objective' or 'value free'?

Can you pick out places where values enter into his measurement of poverty?

What implications does this have for his research?

The questionnaire

The main survey took the form of a thirty-nine page questionnaire which was carried out by trained interviewers. There were nine sections to the questionnaire, which had been identified as important in the pilot research:

- housing and living facilities;
- employment;
- occupational facilities and fringe benefits;
- cash income;
- assets and savings;
- health and disability;
- social services;
- private income in kind;
- styles of living.

Townsend wanted a complete picture of each individual's lifestyle and resources. For his purposes, for example, income included not just income from employment and assets or savings but also private income in kind (e.g. from gardening) and an estimation of financial gain from social services. Many of these things are very difficult to measure and there was often a need for 'elaborate interviewing and editing procedures'.

Clearly the skills of the interviewer are absolutely crucial in obtaining reliable information. It is important that all interviewers are interpreting questions and answers in the same way, otherwise information from different people is not comparable. The research team therefore set up its own interviewing organisation and lengthy briefing conferences were held for interviewers who were also, where possible, involved in pilot interviewing before the main survey. Interviewers were also given very detailed notes on how to ask and how to record answers to every question. There was a core group of twenty-five interviewers although there were others who did not stay throughout the period of research.

■ **Why did Townsend choose a formal interview rather than a questionnaire?**

The following questions and notes to the interviewer should give some idea of both the complexity of the questions and of the importance of the interviewer. The answers given were recorded by the interviewer in the precoded boxes alongside each question and were later fed into a computer to allow statistical analysis.

Question 32 Section 4 was designed to measure private income from gardening etc.

32. Do you grow any of your own food or keep poultry either in the garden or grounds by the home or elsewhere? *

yes, own ground/garden} ASK
yes, allotment, etc } Q.
elsewhere } 32(a)

no }
DK } SKIP TO Q.33

(a) How much a week on average do you think you save yourself and your family by eating or using the things you grow - I mean the price in the shops of the things you use at home, but deducting all your costs and expenses?
NOTE ANY VARIATION IN YEAR ———————— amount ———— per week

QUESTION 32   Value of own food or poultry

Try to obtain a weekly average of the value of using own garden, allotment and farm produce. Do not waste too much time on produce amounting in value to less than 10s. a week. Be careful not to give an inflated estimate of the saving. Husbands sometimes exaggerate the value of what they grow in a large garden. What you want is an estimate of what it would cost in the shops to purchase the kind of produce consumed in the home which is grown by the household, LESS all expenses. For a small-holding or farm this means taking account of purchases of stock or seed, wages, payments of fuel bills, etc., in the same way as earlier you explored the income of the self-employed.

10s (shillings) is equal to 50p

Question 11 Section 3 was designed to measure any financial gain from employment other than actual income:

11. Does your employer provide you with anything else which is of value to you which you have not already told me about?

PROMPT
- any goods free or at reduced prices (e.g. free/concessionary coal or railway tickets)
- travel other than for work
- medical expenses (including medical insurance)
- educational expenses – for your children
- educational expenses – for yourself
- shares or options to purchase shares
- life insurance
- loans or grants towards purchase of car
- other (SPECIFY) _____
- none of these

IF ANY RECORDED
Roughly how much a year are these things worth to you altogether? I mean, how much more would you have to spend if you had bought the same things yourself?

WRITE IN ESTIMATES FOR ITEMS

ENTER TOTAL ANNUAL ESTIMATE IN £'s

QUESTION 11   Other benefits

Read the prompts slowly: they are carefully drafted to cover the perks of both senior and junior staff. **The goods** may vary from free or subsidised coal given to miners to discounts on goods bought or free vegetables, seeds or seedlings. Don't hesitate to pursue it further according to occupations of informants. **Transport** may be free leisure travel given to railway or bus employees or paid holidays given to senior executives. Note this section is supplementary to the use of a vehicle in Q. 10. **Medical expenses** may be premiums to insurance agencies for private medical care or the direct payment of doctors' bills. **Education** can range from free tennis lessons or typing lessons to payment of public school fees. **Shares in the company** can be given free or below market value.

ENCOURAGE THE INFORMANT to add items under the various headings together and give time for this to be done. We are interested to know what it would cost to buy these things privately even though the employee might not have chosen to do so (e.g. the employee might have used the Health Service if his employer did not pay for him to have private medical care).

"How much a year are these things worth altogether?"

The point here is that some kinds of entries will be money saved, say, on goods and services which the informant would have had to pay for, whereas other entries will involve things he would never have afforded or thought about. Our aim is to discover what equivalent in extra income would be needed if he did the same things but had to bear the full cost himself.

■ **Why did the questions need to be pre-coded in this way?**

■ **What difficulties might people experience in answering these questions?**

Both of these questions require the interviewee to have a fairly exact knowledge of the monetary value of certain goods and services and require a skilled interviewer to interpret and thus code the answers.

Townsend does recognise the way in which both the questions asked and the interviewer's approach can significantly affect the results. He says 'In general, the design of the questionnaire and the style adopted by the interviewer "structures" the information that it is possible to collect in a survey.'

Selecting a random sample

Because the aim of the survey was to gain a general picture of the extent and type of poverty in Britain it was important to have a random sample which was representative of the population as a whole.

Townsend used a stratified multi-stage technique. It was impractical to survey the whole country so areas were selected first (multi-stage) but Townsend wanted to be sure that he included all income areas, therefore for the first stage of sampling, areas were stratified into high/middle and low income areas. The population of selected areas was then further stratified according to age and family size. Multi-stage sampling makes research easier to carry out avoiding the need to travel all over the country. Stratified sampling is an attempt to make your sample as representative as possible of the population being studied. To check the representativeness of his sample

■ **Why is it important to have a random sample for this research?**

Townsend compared his sample with the population of Britain as a whole from the Registrar General's figures. He found his sample to be very representative.

The overall response rate to the survey was high, nearly 76 per cent of households gave complete information and a total of 82 per cent participated completely or partially.

Non-response was felt to be potentially a large problem since it is to be expected that the elderly, the disabled etc. are more likely to figure amongst non-respondents. Interviewers were therefore instructed to call back.

For the 388 households who refused an interview, interviewers filled out a special form giving the limited information that was available. For most non-respondents, for example, it was possible to determine whether the house was rented or owner-occupied, the age of the householders and the social class of the head of household.

Information about non-respondents is also more important to collect than in many other surveys. Relatively more of the sick, the aged and those with large numbers of children are likely to have difficulty in granting an interview. Yet relatively more of them are likely to be poor. We must ensure that our estimates of the incidence of poverty are not weakened by lack of information about non-respondents in the sample. We are, therefore, instructing interviewers to do all that is humanly possible to record vital information about the composition of the household, housing amenities and other matters.

Why might the fact that old people and disabled people are less likely to reply be a problem for Townsend's research?

Results

In 1968-9 Townsend argued that 25 per cent of households (22.9 per cent of the people surveyed, i.e. 12.46 million people) suffered from relative poverty. This estimation of the problem is significantly greater than the figures provided by the DHSS based on supplementary benefits claimants.

Percentages in poverty and on the margins of poverty according to three standards.

Poverty standard	Percentage of households	Percentage of population	Estimated number (UK)	
			Households	Non-institu-tionalized population
State's standard (SB):*				
in poverty	7.1	6.1	1.34 mil.	3.32 mil.
on margins of poverty	23.8	21.8	4.50 mil.	11.86 mil.
Relative income standard:†				
in poverty	10.6	9.2	2.00 mil.	5.0 mil.
on margins of poverty	29.5	29.6	5.58 mil.	16.10 mil.
Deprivation standard:‡				
in poverty	25.2	22.9	4.76 mil.	12.46 mil.
Total (UK)	100	100	18.90 mil.	54.4 mil.

DEFINITIONS:
* Net disposable household income last year of less than 100 per cent (in poverty) or 100 to 139 per cent (on margins of poverty) of supplementary benefit scale rates plus housing costs.
† Net disposable household income last year less than 50 per cent (in poverty) or 50 to 79 per cent (on margins of poverty) of mean household income for type.
‡ Net disposable household income last year of less than a level below which deprivation tends to increase disproportionately as income diminishes.

How might statistical data like this be used?

Townsend isolated several groups of people who were at 'high risk':

1. One-person households
2. Large families
3. Lower class people who tended to work in poor conditions
4. The unemployed
5. The disabled
6. One-parent families
7. Old people

Housing and living conditions were investigated by Townsend's research

Conclusion

'The chief conclusions of this report is that poverty is more extensive than is generally or officially believed and has to be understood not only as an inevitable feature of severe social inequality but also as a particular consequence of actions by the rich to preserve and enhance their wealth and so deny it to others. Control of wealth and the institutions created by that wealth, and . . . of the terms under which it is generated and passed on is central to any policies designed to abolish or alleviate the "condition".'

What does this conclusion tell you about Townsend's own values?

How do you feel they might have influenced his research?

Peter Willmott: *Friendship Networks and Social Support*

This is a small scale social survey which investigates the informal social supports available to people from different social classes and to males and females. Willmott is interested in the role of friends, and to a lesser extent relatives and neighbours, in people's lives in Britain today. Rather than identifying patterns in the population as a whole, which would require a large-scale national survey, Willmott wanted to identify factors which influenced friendship patterns. He was particularly interested in finding out if class or gender affected friendship patterns. In order to look closely at these variables he needed to choose a sample which was fairly homogeneous (similar) in other respects.

Why does Willmott want a sample of people at the same stage in their life, excluding for example single-parent families or families with grandparents living with them?

> The aim therefore was not a sample representative of the general population of Britain (or some part of it) but rather a sample of people particularly suitable for comparison, highlighting crucial differences.
>
> Because the interviews were to be complex and lengthy, the number carried out had to be small. The sample therefore needed to be relatively homogeneous. Hence the decision to interview married people in households containing one or more children under 16.

Selecting the sample

To obtain roughly equal numbers of middle-class and working-class people, two adjacent housing areas in outer London were chosen, 'one a council estate, the other an area of fairly high quality owner-occupied housing'. Households which fulfilled the requirements of the sample were selected from these areas and to provide a sex balance, a statistical method was developed to ensure that roughly equal numbers of males and females were selected from each area.

The sampling technique was not totally successful, since there were more middle-class people living on the council estate and more working-class people living in the other area than had been anticipated. Also, the middle-class area contained a large number of Jews. When this was discovered early in the research attempts were made to include no more Jews in the sample, but Jewish people still amounted to a quarter of those interviewed in the private area and this might have influenced the results since Jewish families are often very closely knit.

How could Willmott have collected a more representative sample?

These and other limitations of the sample made generalisation to the population as a whole difficult.

> It should be made clear, if it is not already, that the 163 people interviewed do not constitute a sample of the population of Britain, of London, of the particular suburb or even of the two areas within it. Those areas, being adjacent to each other, can properly be combined and viewed as a distinct place – an identifiable segment of suburban London – but the people seen were at only one stage in life and the sample was biased towards the British-born white Gentiles living in that particular district. At the same time it is obvious that, just as with earlier local studies of social relationships, the members of the sample can properly be seen as in some sense representative of other people like themselves. The important thing is that the reader should bear in mind the limitations of the study.

The pilot survey

Before the interviews were carried out Willmott conducted 31 pilot interviews on the basis of which some questions were rewritten or excluded. For example, one area of concern was how tightly knit people's networks were, i.e. how far their friends and relatives knew each other. In the final survey this was measured for friends but not relatives.

> . . . we did not feel able to ask about mutual links between all relatives and between relatives and friends in the way we asked about links between friends. One of the problems in the pilot interviews had been that people could not see the point of our asking whether their relatives were independently in touch with each other: 'Of course they all know each other', respondents sometimes complained,'why are we going through all this?' It was because of this particular difficulty, together with a general desire to avoid too long and tedious an interview, that the precise questions about mutual links, and the analysis of these, were confined to friends – the main focus of the study.

Carrying out the research

Interviews were finally carried out with 163 people representing the different classes and males and females in roughly equal numbers. The overall response rate was 59 per cent. A team of five women interviewers and Peter Willmott himself conducted the interviews.

■ **How might having six different interviewers be a problem?**

An initial problem for this research was how to measure concepts like friends and neighbours since there is no agreed definition of these terms, yet for comparison to be possible it is necessary that different respondents attach the same meaning to questions.

> There is thus a fundamental difficulty. How can the relevance of friends to informal support be sensibly examined if there is no agreement about who they are?
>
> We asked about people who had been 'met socially', explaining that we meant something more than 'just saying "Hello" or passing the time of day'. Interviewers were briefed to exclude 'purely casual or trivial contacts'. But I had deliberately not restricted contacts to those which were pre-arranged or those which took place inside people's homes, because to do so might have biased the findings against the friendships of people who did not organise their social lives in such ways.
>
> As it was, the definitions used were hardly exact. Though most respondents seemed to have no difficulty in understanding the terminology or applying it to their own experience, the questioning was still dependent on people's own interpretation of the key words. So some friends will certainly have been excluded who should have been included and vice-versa, and the risk remains that to this extent different things are being compared in later chapters.

■ **How might this affect the results?**

The questionnaire included 72 questions. All except for the last eight of these were closed and were coded to allow computer analysis. The interviewers were given detailed instructions on how to code the responses. For example:

36. What sort of thing do you do when you see your relatives?
    RECORD AND CODE ONE ONLY IN PRIORITY ORDER

	40
Meals in	1
Meals out	2
Drinks in	3
Drinks out	4
Tea/coffee	5
Outside leisure (walking, fishing, dancing, theatre, cinema etc)	6
Just talk/chat	7
Other	8

■ **What are the advantages of asking closed questions like these? What are the main problems?**

■ Why do you feel that a
formal interview rather
than a questionnaire was
used to conduct this
survey?

In addition, basic details on all people named by each respondent were recorded on a person-form providing easily analysable information on all people met socially by each person interviewed.

Findings

The survey produced a mass of statistical data which enabled Willmott to discuss the contact with friends and neighbours and relatives of people from different class backgrounds and different sexes. He was also able to see how other factors such as education, car ownership, and private housing affected friendship patterns and look at the types of support received from different sorts of people. With the exception of one section, on the meaning of friendship, results were all presented in statistical form and were tested to see if they could have been achieved by chance. So for example, Willmott found that people on average identified 23 friends, although this varied from three to 58. Generally there was no difference between males and females but middle-class people, those living in private housing, those with a higher level of education and those who owned their own cars tended to have more social contacts than working-class people. However, if frequency of contacts was taken into account, working-class people had no less contacts than middle-class people. Contact with relatives over a six month period was not significantly different between the classes but working-class people had more contact with their relatives on a weekly basis, with an average of 3.37 contacts per week compared to 2.08 contacts for middle-class people and with 78 per cent of working-class people as compared to 58 per cent of middle-class people seeing at least one relative at least once a week.

People also used relatives and friends in different circumstances, as shown in the table below. (The figures are the percentage of people offering that kind of help.)

Sources of eight kinds of help

	Relative	Friend	Neighbour	Other person
Child's illness	64	32	3	1
Babysitting	70	20	3	7
Shopping	37	55	8	–
House maintenance	33	54	13	–
'Keeping an eye on house'	21	47	31	1
Financial advice	75	22	–	3
Financial loan	78	19	–	3
Personal advice	42	56	–	2

Relatives also became less important as people became older.

Reliance on relatives for help, by respondent's age

	Percentages in each category	
	29 or under	30 or over
Citing relatives as source in:		
Child's illness	85	61
Babysitting	81	66
Shopping	65	28
House maintenance	30	32
'Keeping an eye on house'	48	13
Financial advice	94	68
Financial loan	99	73
Personal advice	65	35

■ What type of data is
produced from this
survey?

What are the uses of this
type of data? What are the
limitations?

27

Working-class people were slightly more reliant on relatives than middle-class people.

The majority of the book is an attempt to measure, statistically, factors which influence the role of relatives, neighbours and friends in the lives of the British population. There is also an attempt to measure the meaning of friendship to respondents. This required somewhat different questions from the closed questions used elsewhere.

For example:

What sort of research could you do to discover the *meaning* of friends and relatives to people's lives?

68. What kinds of things do you think lead to you becoming friendly wIth people in the first place?

70. I asked earlier what you meant by the word 'neighbour'. What do you think is the difference between someone you'd call a 'neighbour' and a 'friend'?

There is, again, an attempt to classify the answers and identify patterns.

QUESTIONS

1. **What are the advantages of conducting a pilot survey? Use examples to illustrate your answer.**

2. **What type of data is provided by social surveys? What are the uses and limitations of this type of research? Illustrate with reference to either or both of the studies.**

3. **Taking into account the nature of the sampling and the response rate, to what extent is it possible to generalise from each of these studies?**

4. **Townsend says 'The question is not just whether the sample who are successfully interviewed represent the population but whether the information provided by them was of uniformly reliable quality'. Using the examples of questions given, why might some answers be unreliable? (Consider the demands on both the interviewer and interviewee.)**

5. **Both of these studies used a formal interview. Can you identify the advantages of this? When might it be preferable to use a postal questionnaire?**

6. **'Values must inevitably enter research in many ways, from the choice of topics to be studied, through the formulation of hypotheses, and the methodology adopted, to the final interpretation of the data.' (AEB 1981) Discuss this statement with reference to Townsend's and Willmott's research.**

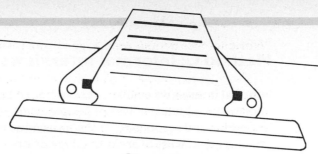

Checklist

ADVANTAGES

1. At a practical level the social survey is quick and cheap to conduct when compared to methods such as participant observation.

2. Pre-coded, standardised questions make it possible to analyse surveys quickly and accurately on a computer.

3. Because questions are standardised it is possible to identify patterns and make comparisons between different groups of people such as between males and females or between working class and middle class.

4. If the sampling is successful it is possible to make general statements to the population as a whole rather than just about the group being studied.

5. Social surveys are verifiable, they could be carried out by someone else to check the reliability of the results. They could also be carried out again at a future date in order to make comparisons over time.

6. In questionnaires, because the interviewer is not present there is no problem of interviewer bias. In structured or formal interviews this problem may be minimal since identical questions are simply read out (although tone of voice, etc. may influence interviewees.)

DISADVANTAGES

1. If the sample is large analysis might be time consuming, producing results which are already out of date.

2. Statistics give no indication of individual meaning or interpretation.

3. Premature closure of questions means that people may often only be able to give an approximation of their feelings; the answer they want may not be there.

4. It might be argued that no questions are truly standardised. People may attach a different meaning to, and interpret the same question in totally different ways. This makes comparison of answers difficult especially if particular groups have a common interpretation.

5. Results may be decided by the way in which the concepts are defined and measured by the researcher and the way in which the questions are asked. For example, Townsend's definition of poverty produced very different results from surveys which have defined and measured poverty differently.

6. It is difficult to check whether people are answering honestly.

7. If the sampling is less than random or if the response rate is low, the findings will be less reliable.

◼ Using the checklist, give examples of these pros and cons from Willmott's and Townsend's research.

◼ **PROJECT**

Either select a research question from pages 77-79, or write your own question that lends itself to the survey method of enquiry. Consider whether a formal interview, group questionnaire (as for example in a classroom) or postal questionnaire is most suitable.

For one of your chosen areas write and pilot a list of questions. Include a variety of different types of questions including open and closed questions and questions on attitudes and knowledge.

Method C: Informal Interviews

Informal interviews enable a researcher to gain detailed and descriptive information about the lives of people being studied. The interviewer must be flexible and responsive to the interviewee, guiding the conversation with either a general list of areas to cover or open-ended questions. The aim is to encourage the interviewee to talk freely, allowing them to determine the important aspects of the discussion. Often tape recorders are used to ensure that the information is a true record of the interview which can be referred back to and analysed at a later date. Because of the detail involved, informal interviews are usually carried out on a smaller sample of people than social surveys. This, together with the open nature of the questions, makes it difficult to generalise from the findings. The two examples of informal interviews in this chapter study personal issues for which a great deal of trust between interviewer and interviewee is necessary. Both studies use some structured questions to gain basic factual information, although most questions are informal.

Ann Oakley: *From Here to Maternity*

■ **Why is this topic suited to research by informal interviews rather than a) a questionnaire, or b) participant observation?**

The aim of this book was to look at the experience of becoming a mother in modern British society. Oakley argues that this, rather than marriage, is the point at which gender has most impact on women's lives.

> Whereas 50 or even 20 years ago women gave up their jobs on marriage, now they do so during their first pregnancies, and it is the moment when she becomes a mother that a woman first confronts the full reality of what it means to be a woman in our society. Motherhood entails a great deal of domestic work – servicing the child, keeping its clothes and its body clean, preparing food. The demarcation lines between this and house- or husband-work blur. It is a crisis in the life of a woman, a point of no return. Evidence accumulated since the 1950s about how the principle of sex equality works in practice shows conclusively that the options available for women outside the home are severely affected by motherhood, and remain so even where 'officially' the commitment is to equal chances for all.
>
> I therefore chose to look at this moment in a woman's history, to catch it and describe it and explore it through the eyes of some of those who experience it. I was interested in every dimension of becoming a mother: changes in life-style – giving up work, staying at home, becoming isolated or making new friends – the impact of, and effect on, marriage, the relationship between mother and child, the medical management of childbirth. I wanted to show that the advent of motherhood is not only an event of importance to the individual woman, but a moment in the history of *all* women.

Oakley's interest in this topic is both academic and personal, she makes no claims to scientific objectivity in her choice of topic:

> I am a feminist, an academic sociologist, and a woman with children. I was not a feminist until I had children, and I became a sociologist as an escape from the problems of having children. My first child was born in 1967 when I was 22 and had accomplished a university degree, various minor pieces of research for other people and two unpublished novels. I thought it was my vocation as a woman to be a mother. When my son was 16 months old, my first daughter was

born. Both children seemed to me absolutely lovely, and I delighted in them both, but the time that followed was an unhappy haze of nappy-washing and pill-taking, as I found I could not make my dream of domestic contentment come true. I felt depressed and oppressed. I felt constantly tired, I felt isolated, I felt resentful of my husband's freedom, I felt my life was at an end. The pills did not adjust me to my role. In those days – the late 1960s – it was not yet acceptable for women to admit openly to their dissatisfactions. Eventually it dawned on me (and I cannot now remember how) that perhaps I both could and should do something else. I registered to do a doctoral thesis and embarked on my research on housewives. Almost at the same time I encountered two women who were starting a women's liberation group in my area. Joining them I began to understand how my private conflicts were nothing more or less than the legacy that all women in modern industrialised society inherit.

She discusses her own experiences of childbirth at length, concluding:

> This personal testimony is, of course, not intended to be definitive, there are many ways of having a baby. The point is that academic research projects bear an intimate relationship to the researcher's life, however 'scientific' a sociologist pretends to be. Personal dramas provoke ideas that generate books and research projects.

Can you identify ways in which Oakley's biases might influence her research?

Personal commitment to a research project inevitably presents problems:

> There were times in the course of the research when I began to confuse my roles – researcher, pregnant woman, mother, feminist, participant observer and so on. I found such confusion disturbing but healthy, for it indicates the artificiality of the boundaries we set ourselves. Human experience is often not as neat and tidy as we strive to make it.

Prior to the main research Oakley spent six months as an observer in the London hospital from which she chose her sample of women. The study itself is based upon intensive interviews with 66 women:

> Four interviews were carried out with each woman – at average times of 26 weeks and six weeks before delivery, and five weeks and 20 weeks afterwards. I also attended six of the births. By the time interview four arrived, the numbers had fallen to 55: four women miscarried, one had the baby prematurely at another hospital, five moved too far away to be interviewed again, and one withdrew from the project because of a disintegrating marriage. All the interviews were tape-recorded and lasted on average 2.36 hours.

Selecting the sample

The sample was selected to enable general points to be made about the experiences of first-time motherhood and therefore certain groups of people were excluded. Confining the sample to one hospital inevitably presented problems of representativeness:

> I chose a sample of women who were all booked for delivery in the same hospital because I did not want to end up comparing the practices of different hospitals: this would have confused the main point of the research, which was to arrive at a picture of those experiences of first-time motherhood that are shared by all women.
>
> The women were aged between 19 and 32 at the time of delivery. I intended to look at first at birth when it happens to most women in our society – the average age for having a first child is now 25 years in Britain and 22 years in the United States. All the women were born in Britain, Ireland or North America; I did not include ethnic minorities, since what research is available on reproductive attitudes shows these to vary with different cultural groups. To compare these would have been an entire research project on its own.

According to husband's occupation, the conventional sociological index, 64 per cent of the women interviewed were middle class, 36 per cent working class. According to the woman's own occupation, the figures are 91 per cent middle class and 9 per cent working class; two thirds of the middle-class mothers had social-class III non-manual occupations. This is a more middle-class population than is representative of the pattern nationally, and reflects the patient population of that particular hospital. Eleven per cent of the women were not married at the first interview, 7 per cent were still not married by the last interview. I saw no reason to exclude unmarried mothers: 9 per cent of births in Britain in 1976 and 14 per cent in the USA in 1975 were to unmarried mothers.

How appropriate is it to generalise from Oakley's findings to women having their first baby?

Carrying out the interviews

The interviews were all conducted by Oakley herself and included a number of very open questions which encouraged the interviewees to discuss their own feelings fully. Some of these questions were extremely personal in nature. Questions were followed up with supplementary questions when this seemed appropriate. Some of the more general questions included:

- Did you want a baby?
- When you found out definitely that you were pregnant, how did you feel about it?
- Do you enjoy being pregnant?
- How much do you think you know about looking after babies?
- Can you describe your feelings when you first held the baby?
- What sort of person is your baby?
- Why do you want to breast/bottle feed?
- Do you feel that the baby has affected your marriage?

The majority of the text consists of women talking:

> When I came to confront the completed interviews I was impressed by the fact that the women said it all much better, and much more clearly and directly, than a sociologist could ever do. I decided to put together a book that consisted as much as possible of the women's own words, to allow them to present their own accounts of pregnancy, birth and the experiences of early motherhood.

Oakley does additionally present some simplified statistics in an attempt to identify general patterns, particularly on factual issues such as use of pain killers during birth, breastfeeding etc. The following extracts should give some idea of the type of data which was produced.

- Has the pregnancy been anything like you expected?

Feelings about pregnancy	
Better than expected	46%
Worse than expected	36%
Same/don't know	18%

Nina Brady:
No. What did I expect it to be like? I didn't expect to be so awkward. I'm very awkward. Fat and that. Very fat. I'm over twelve stone. You bump into everything. And he's afraid to turn at night for fear he'll hit me with an elbow or something. I didn't expect to be so tired. I thought I'd be able to work till about six weeks before but I couldn't.

Elizabeth Farell:
Yes. Well it's been perfect really. Because I haven't been interfered with at all – you know, it hasn't *inhibited* me at all.

• Can you describe your feelings when you first held the baby?

Feelings on first holding the baby	
Not interested	70%
Amazed, proud	20%
Euphoric	10%

Sasha Morris had an epidural, but she used the phrase 'completely numbed' to describe her emotional reaction:
I was absolutely stunned. I couldn't say that I felt anything for her for a while. The next day I was reluctant to admit it to anyone – I said oh I was delighted, but I wasn't . . . and of course Ben was very moved by the whole thing. He had tears in his eyes which is most unusual for him, because he's a very tough businessman – he wouldn't have tears in his eyes for anybody, he's not the emotional sort, but he was *extremely* moved. Which pleased me: I was delighted by his reaction. But I had none of my own. I felt nothing. I couldn't relate myself to her at all. And I never asked if she was alright. I said *nothing*. Everybody said she's a girl. I though oh: how tremendous. When I looked at her I thought she was lovely. When I held her I said to Ben, you take her. I didn't want to hold her for a long time. And when they took her away I wasn't saying where are you going with her? And I think the same night they brought her for a feed and I put her beside me and I thought she was lovely, but I didn't want to pick her up and hug her. I just wanted to go to sleep. And I couldn't. I was so tired.

I was very amazed at my own reaction when she was born. I was completely *numbed*. I thought I'd be delighted. I think a lot of people won't admit to their feelings. They say they're absolutely delighted, but I'm sure half of them aren't. It's quite normal, isn't it?

Dawn O'Hara:
Oh cripey. It was the best moment of my life. You know if I ever see that advertisement for Sterling Health on television it brings back memories, you know? I could cry!

■ **What are the advantages and disadvantages of 'letting women speak for themselves' rather than asking standardised questions?**

■ **How can bias enter into a structured interview?**

At the end of the book Oakley discusses interviews as a method of gaining sociological information. She argues that the interview is often presented as a clinical research tool, by which an objective interviewer asks questions of a passive interviewee. The answers can then be used to compare people and identify patterns. The process of interviewing – neither the nature of the questions asked nor the interaction between interviewer and interviewee – supposedly has an influence on the data produced. On the contrary, she argues that the interview is inevitably a reactive research tool which itself can change reality.

For once you start to study people it is at least a possibility that they become so influenced by the fact of being studied that their behaviour or attitudes are changed, and the whole point of doing the research is lost.

For, contrary to what the textbooks say, researching and being researched are parts of *human* interaction; it may be wishful thinking (or unnecessary pessimism) to think that they can be governed entirely by 'scientific' principles. One feature of these 545 hours 26 minutes of tape-recorded human conversations is the tendency of the interviewed to ask questions back. In all, the tapes include 878 such questions. For example:
Does ultrasound hurt the baby?

Can you refuse induction?
Who will deliver my baby?
Does the epidural ever paralyse you?
Is it right that the baby doesn't come out of the same hole you pass water out of?
How will I know when I'm in labour?
What is the pain of birth like?
Is breastfeeding sexual?
How long should you wait for sex after the birth?
Can my baby see yet?
Do disposable nappies go down the lavatory?
Does shaking the child harm it?
How do you cook an egg for a baby?
Do you have periods when you're breastfeeding?
What's the difference between the coil and the cap?
How do you clean the baby's nails?
What causes cot death?

Oakley always answered the questions. Interviewing is therefore a two-way process. At the end of the interview she asked all of her interviewees 'Do you feel that being involved in this research – my coming to see you – has affected your experience of becoming a mother in any way?' A summary of the replies and some actual examples are included below:

Has the research affected your experience of becoming a mother?	
No	27%
Yes:	73%
thought about it more	30%*
found it reassuring	25%*
a relief to talk	30%*
changed attitudes/ behaviour	7%*

* Percentages do not add up to 100 per cent because some women gave more than one answer.

Clare Dawson:
It's made me think about things that I've never thought about before. For instance, when you said to me does it matter to you if you don't see the same doctor? And I began to think: I wonder if it does? At the time I said no. And then I thought about it more. And I suppose it made me *assess* more what happened. I think I've found it helpful, actually. To talk about it: it's been good to talk about it . . . I think it would be interesting to see what other people thought or felt. I can't see what *can* come out of it, in a way, because everybody's so different. I can't see how you can compare . . .

Pauline Diggory:
It's been very, I've really *enjoyed* it. Yes, it has helped me because I probably would have been even more worried. I mean, I think you know a lot. I mean there you are with all these different mothers and I mean all I've got to say is, do you think Hannah's a bit sick and you say, oh no, I've seen about so many . . . Now that just helps, just to say you've seen a few.
Ann Oakley: But of course I'm not a doctor.
Pauline: Oh I know. But I mean a doctor's not interested in a baby being sick anyway.

During the course of the interviews Oakley clearly developed a relationship with her interviewees. It could be argued that this had both positive and negative effects. Discuss these.

Dobash & Dobash: *Violence Against Wives 1980*

Dobash & Dobash attempt to describe and explain wife battering in modern society. They argue that contrary to general belief, the family is not a secure, happy and peaceful place. They write:

> The fact is that for most people, and especially for women and children, the family is the most violent group to which they are likely to belong. Despite fears to the contrary, it is not a stranger but a so-called loved one who is most likely to assault, rape, or murder us.

Violence against wives is seen as an extension of men's domination and control over women which has been historically and socially constructed. Religious, literary and legal writings are seen as presenting women only in terms of their relationships to men, i.e. wives, mothers and daughters. This, coupled with the power given to men through many social institutions (e.g. political, economic) has resulted in family life being an area of male authority over women.

Socialisation ensures that women's actions are restricted and orientated to serve men. Dobash & Dobash write:

> Females are 'born' to be wives. To be a 'real' woman requires becoming a wife and to be a complete wife means being a good mother. Nothing less is really acceptable and little more is tolerated. Women are circumscribed by this, the only truly legitimate status they are allowed, and all of their activities are in some ways restricted by it and defined in terms of it. Women, in their position as wives, become relatively separated from the world and isolated in the home, where they are meant to be subordinate to their husbands and to serve the needs of others. This situation is part of the cultural legacy of the patriarchal family. There have, of course, been numerous historical changes in the status of women and in the institution of marriage: wife beating is no longer strictly legal and an absolute patriarchy can no longer be said to exist. Most of these changes, however, have done little to modify the patriarchal ideals and hierarchical nature of family organization. They continue. The beliefs are taught to all children and there are numerous means by which we institutionalize and legitimate the control that husbands have over their wives.

What does this tell us about Dobash and Dobash's perspective?

Dobash & Dobash therefore feel that little information is really available about violence against wives. The 'commonsense' explanations such as, 'she must have deserved it', 'they obviously like it', etc. are completely unacceptable. They argue:

> What is required is in-depth information about the violence itself and the relationship in which it occurs, as well as an analysis of the society in which wife beating occurs and the cultural beliefs and institutional practices that contribute to this pattern.

The pilot study

In order to do this they first conducted a pilot study:

> . . . both to aid in the development of an interview schedule for a more extensive study of wife beating and to allow for the discovery of factors not included in our initial conception of the problem.

These interviews were with battered women and people who had worked with violent families (for example social workers, police officers, organisers of refuges for battered women). Using 'orientating questions' and later an interview guide, they asked open-ended questions on topics such as

socialisation into the use of violence, differentials of status between husban
and wife, use of alcohol, and husband/wife expectations.

Selecting the sample

The main study involved 109 interviews with women who had experienced
battering. 67 of these were living in refuges for battered women in
Edinburgh and Glasgow, 26 were living in refuges in smaller towns in
Scotland and 16 had recently left a refuge. The women came from
working-class and middle-class backgrounds, ranging in age from 16 to 60.
The majority of women were between 21 and 30. Most of them had two or
three children. Women were usually interviewed within a few days of their
arrival at the refuge. No one who was asked refused to take part. They write

■ **What effect will these
considerations have on
the nature of the sample?**

> We purposely chose a sample of battered women who were willing to speak in
> considerable detail about what is for many people an unspeakable and
> unsharable problem.

Carrying out the interviews

The majority of the interviews were conducted by two female research
assistants who spent many months in continual contact with the refuge.

> The research assistants were not mere interviewers but rather became
> permanent fixtures in the life and activities of the refuges. They spent
> considerable time in the refuges apart from the time engaged in interviewing and
> often were sympathetic listeners to women concerned about their present
> predicament and future prospects. The researchers were not strangers but
> people with histories that were learned by the newcomers to the refuges from
> those who were already residing in them for a period of time and who had been
> previously interviewed by ourselves or Cavanagh and Wilson. This continual
> contact with the refuges had the unintended but important consequence of
> developing considerable trust between the interviewers and the women, which
> in most cases meant good rapport during interviews.

■ **What are the advantages
and disadvantages of this?**

All the interviews were taped and varied in length between 2–12 hours. An
informal approach was adopted with standardised questions, which
interviewers could change or clarify if they felt it was appropriate.

> This open-ended technique increases the probability of the interviewer's
> understanding 'the context of the answers, perceptions or motivations' of
> respondents.

Most interviews began by the women being asked about their family
background, their education, childhood and any early experiences of
violence. This introduced the conversation into the realm of courtship and
marriage, with some time being spent exploring any changes in their
relationship. Women were specifically asked about the first, the worst and
the last experience of violence they had experienced. For example: 'Can you
tell me about the first time your husband hit you?' They write:

> We then asked specific questions regarding the violent event. Each of these
> discrete episodes, the first, worst, and last, was discussed in terms of when it
> occurred, the circumstances preceding the violence, the physical nature of the
> attack, its location, the presence of others during the attack, the extent and
> severity of injuries, and the immediate responses and feelings of the husband
> and wife. When women were allowed to talk about these incidents in their own
> words, as well as to answer our more specific questions, they gave very detailed
> accounts of even those incidents that had occurred many years earlier.

■ **Why might this
information be important?**

In cases where the women did not talk freely and in detail about their experiences an interviewer would probe further. For example:

Can you remember what actually led up to the first time he hit you then? I mean, as you say, it was . . .

It's only now that I remember back. It's just that we used to sit and quarrel and he'd end up going for me. I don't know. I used to feel he was very jealous and I couldn't wear makeup or anything if I got all dressed up and that. That's how the arguments used to start. I hadn't even sort of gone out, but I'd maybe feel like doing myself up. He'd start hitting me, you know.

And can you remember what happened that first time? How he hit you? Was it just a punch?

He just punched me under the chin actually. I seen stars.

Was it just the once the first time?

Uh-huh.

Did you hit him back?

I was too astounded. I'd never been hit before, so I was just standing there for the short time that I had to take it.

And can you recall what time of day this was?

It was always, nearly always, night-time.

And did it happen in your house?

Well, at the time, yes, it was a house.

Can you recall, was it the living room, or the kitchen, or the bedroom?

It was in the living room.

And was it just the two of you or were the kids there?

No, there was people in the house at the time.

There were other people there? Were they relatives or friends?

No, just friends.

And what did they do when he hit you?

They all started edging up, quite honestly, 'cos the girls started screaming, a couple of girls that were in, and the men that were his pals stood. They were used to seeing things like that.

They didn't try and pull him off you?

They used to tell him to stop, but he didn't take any notice. I don't think they really bothered.

And were you hurt at all after that? I mean, apart from the shock?

Well, I couldn't believe in that he just hit me, you know. I didn't feel the same towards him after that.

What skills does an informal interviewer need?

Questions were also asked about what actually happened during a violent episode, and the beliefs and values the participants had in connection with marriage and conjugal roles.

Findings

The use of the open-ended questions allowed Dobash & Dobash to provide a detailed account of the experiences of battered women and to gain some understanding of the meanings of their experiences. This, coupled with the use of some standardised questions enabled them to quantify some of the more common experiences and identify patterns. They discovered that during early courtship the majority of the women in the study had warm, attentive, loving relationships. Where conflict between couples did exist, it commonly centred around the man's sexual jealousy. For example:

Did he ever hit you before you got married?

No. He once got very angry with me. He didn't hit me, but he got very angry. I thought it was because he was fond of me and he was jealous, but I didn't realise until afterwards that it was nothing to do with fondness. It was quite different. He asked me a lot of questions about who I had been out with before I knew him and he made me bring from the house a whole pile of letters and photographs and he stood over me as I stood over an open drain in the road and I had to put them in one by one – tear them up and put them in.

It is the man's sense of possessiveness and exclusivity that seems to develop more strongly during the courtship, and as the relationship moves closer to marriage he has a greater sense of his right to take over the woman and even, as in this case, to try to obliterate, if only in a symbolic sense, all her relationships with anyone other than himself.

23 per cent of the sample did actually experience violence before marriage, but most believed this would cease once they were married. For the majority of the women (77 per cent) there was no indication of the violence to come. Any displays of anger at this stage were often perceived by the women as an indication of how serious the man was about her, rather than any detrimental part of the relationship. Once married the majority of the women spent more time with their husbands and had less contact with family and friends. The husbands however tended to increase the amount of time spent with friends.

Table 1: How frequently the man went out with his own friends throughout the relationship

Frequency	Before Marriage		First Year Marriage		Later Marriage	
	N	%	N	%	N	%
6-7 times per week	14	13	18	17	42	39
1-5 times per week	39	36	59	54	47	43
1-2 times per month	8	7	6	5	0	0
1-6 times per year	3	3	4	4	1	1
Never	45	41	22	20	19	17
Total	109	100	109	100	109	100

As one woman explains, this changing pattern had a very real effect on their relationship.

When we were first married you couldn't find a nicer person, considerate. He couldn't seem to do enough for you. He really was a nice person then. He used to take me to the late-night cinema on Saturday night at the Odeon; apart from that, a few times out to visit his friends in the evening and never anywhere else. I didn't mind going out to the cinema, but I wasn't keen about going to see his friends (because her husband refused to include her in the conversation and his friends ignored her). After we were married he would have to almost be forced to take me out for a drink. . .
He saw his friends quite a lot . . . He used to have two days off and quite often he would say, 'I'm just going to see so-and-so for an hour and I'll be back.' And it would be more like six or seven hours before he turned up again. (When she

told him that she didn't like this, he replied) that this was his only day off and he should get to do what he liked with it.

Also, marriage meant that child rearing, domestic chores and any emotional support was left solely as the responsibility of 'the wife'.

The violent event

The first violent episode usually consisted of a single blow, with little physical injury. It was preceded by an argument, often associated with the husband's possessiveness and his ideas about his wife's responsibility to him. Classically, this incident was followed by shock, shame and guilt, from both parties. The husband begged forgiveness and promised that it wouldn't happen again, while wives often attempted to understand the action in terms of their own behaviour. (The idea that she brought it on herself.)

Tables 2 and 3 give us a picture of how sources of conflict and the nature of the attacks change from the first, worst and last attacks.

Table 2: Sources of conflict leading to violent episodes

| | Violent episode | | | | | | | |
| | First | | Worst | | Last | | Typical | |
Sources of conflict	N	%	N	%	N	%	N	%
Sexual jealousy	31	31	28	30	21	22	48	45
Expectations about domestic work	37	37	32	34	31	32	17	16
Money	7	7	12	13	11	11	18	17
Status problems	3	3	3	3	6	6	3	3
Sexual refusal	6	6	1	1	2	2	2	2
Wife's attempts to leave	5	5	7	7	15	15	0	0
Relatives and friends	3	3	1	1	2	2	4	4
Husband's drinking behavior	1	1	1	1	2	2	7	6
Children	5	5	6	6	6	6	4	4
Other	2	2	4	4	2	2	3	3
Total	100	100	95	100	98	100	106	100

*Table 3: Types of physical force used during violent episodes**

| | Violent episode | | | | | | | |
| | First | | Worst | | Last | | Typical | |
Physical force	N	%	N	%	N	%	N	%
Slap or push/pull into non-injurious object	73	29	48	12	68	21	78	15
Punch face and/or body	85	34	126	33	102	31	226	45
Push/pull into injurious object	27	11	67	17	48	15	19	4
Kick, knee, or butt	39	16	82	21	60	18	140	28
Attempt to drown, smother, or strangle	9	4	20	5	18	5	9	2
Hit with object/weapon	13	5	24	6	17	5	26	5
Other (bite, stand on, rape)	3	1	12	3	18	5	8	1
Total	249	100	389	100	331	100	506	100

What is the value of quantitative information?

* We recorded up to five *different types* of physical force in any single violent episode. These figures reflect only the *different types* of physical force used and not the number of times each type was used.

These tables alone do not provide us with detailed information about the experience of the attack. Dobash & Dobash therefore rely on the descriptions provided by the women:

> He punched me, he kicked me, he pulled me by the hair. My face hit a step. He had his bare feet, you know, with being in bed, and he just jumped up and he pulled on his trousers and he was kicking me. If he had his shoes on, God knows what kind of face I would have had. As it was I had a cracked cheek-bone, two teeth knocked out, cracked ribs, broken nose, two beautiful black eyes – it wasn't even a black eye, it was my whole cheek was just purple from one eye to the other. And he had got me by the neck and, you know, he was trying, in fact, practically succeeded in strangling me. I was choking, I was actually at the blacking-out stage. I was trying to pull his fingers away, with me trying to pull his fingers away, I scratched myself, you know, trying to get his fingers off. He hit me and I felt my head, you know, hitting the back of the lock of the door. I started to scream and I felt as if I'd been screaming for ages. When I came to he was pulling me up the stair by the hair, I mean, I think it was the pain of him pulling me up the stair by the hair that brought me round again. I can remember going up the stair on my hands and knees and the blood – I dinnae know where it was coming from – it was just dripping in front of my face and I was actually covered in blood. I just got to the kitchen door and he just walked straight to his bed. I just filled the sink with cold water, put a dish towel in it, and held it up to my face. I remember I went through to the living room and I fell asleep and I woke up in the morning with this matted dish towel, and, God I couldn't move. There wasn't a bit of me that wasnae sore.

Why are these detailed descriptive accounts of great value to the research?

Few women (only four out of the sample) responded to violence with physical force. The size and strength of the men may have made retaliation very difficult, or there may be complex psychological reasons why the women felt unable to fight back. The types of injuries inflicted upon the women are shown in Table 4.

Table 4: Types of injuries resulting from the first, worst, and last violent episode*

Injuries	Violent episode					
	First		Worst		Last	
	N	%	N	%	N	%
Bruises to face and/or body	101	74	182	64	148	70
Abrasions	0	0	2	1	3	1
Burns	0	0	4	1	5	3
Cuts	18	13	48	17	27	13
Hair torn out	5	3	13	5	10	5
Fractured bones or broken teeth	6	5	11	4	9	4
Internal injuries, miscarriages	4	3	8	3	2	1
Knocked unconscious	2	1	14	5	7	3
Total	136	100	282	100	211	100

* We recorded up to five *different types* of physical injuries in any single violent episode. These figures reflect only the *different types* of injuries, and not the number of times a particular type of injury was received.

Dobash & Dobash found that the majority of attacks (75 per cent) lasted 30 minutes or less. Twenty five per cent of the sample had experienced attacks of 45 minutes to five hours in length. All attacks took place in the home, usually at night-time (between 10-12 p.m.) on a Friday or Saturday night (80 per cent).

A key question is why don't women leave if things are so bad? Dobash & Dobash explored reasons for women staying in order to answer this. From their sample, 88 per cent of the women *had* left at some stage, but went back because of their impossible financial situation – and problems with self-esteem and confidence. Children often rated highly as reasons for both leaving and staying. A fundamental issue for most women was that they would not accept their children being beaten – even if they have been beaten themselves for many years. This was the final straw for most women, and marked the point when they left.

Dobash & Dobash also discovered that most violence goes unreported. From the sample, 32,000 assaults were experienced by the women, of which 517 were reported to the police. Most women remained silent about the violence, even when it was severe, and rarely sought medical attention. This often meant that broken bones healed crookedly, and many women suffered from long term or permanent disfigurement. Table 5 indicates the people most likely to be informed of an attack.

Table 5: Third parties contacted by women after violent episodes

| Third party | Violent episode | | | | | |
| | First | | Worst | | Last | |
	N	%	N	%	N	%
Parent, other relative	37	33	47	19	42	11
Friend	20	18	20	8	33	9
Neighbour	13	11	24	10	23	6
Doctor	21	13	53	22	43	12
Minister	3	3	5	2	3	1
Social Worker	6	5	35	14	63	17
Police	12	11	35	14	47	13
Women's Aid	–	–	14	6	93	25
Other	1	1	13	5	24	6
Total Contacts	113	100	245	100	371	100
Number of Women Making Contacts	52		88		105	

■ QUESTIONS

1. **Both Dobash & Dobash and Oakley taped interviews; what are the advantages and disadvantages of this method?**

2. **To what extent is it possible to generalise from the findings in each of these studies? Explain your answer.**

3. **What alternative methods could be used to investigate (a) women having their first baby, and (b) wife battering? What type of data could be obtained?**

4. **Both researchers present their findings in both a quantitative and a qualitative way. What is the value of this?**

5. **Use these examples to discuss the problem of 'interviewer bias'. Is this just a problem for informal interviews?**

6. **Critics would argue that informal interviews may provide insights but are too subjective and value-laden to be useful for hypothesis testing. How would sociologists who use this method defend their research?**

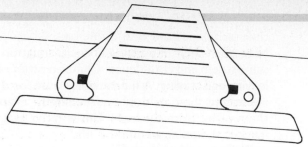

Checklist

ADVANTAGES

1. Often a good deal of rapport develops between interviewer and Interviewee, enabling detailed, honest information to be obtained. This is particularly important where the subject of the research might be regarded as personal or sensitive.

2. It provides an opportunity for people to speak for themselves so that we can get close to people's experiences.

3. The data is not pre-defined by the questions set. The interviewer can follow up leads and gain detailed information.

4. The meanings behind actions can be explored rather than just discovering the facts.

5. If using a tape recorder the information is complete and can be referred back to during analysis.

DISADVANTAGES

1. The 'success' of the interview often rests on the skill of the interviewer.

2. There are 3 problems with interviewer bias: (a) The interviewer may be unconsciously biased, giving non-verbal cues, e.g. frowning, which could influence an interviewee's response; (b) The interviewer may only follow up leads s/he considers to be important. This may be at odds with the interpretation of the people in the study; (c) Where there is more than one interviewer it may be possible that they introduce different biases.

3. It can be time-consuming and expensive and therefore fewer interviews take place.

4. Samples tend to be small with non-standardised questions making generalisations and production of statistics difficult.

5. Refusal to be interviewed can make the sample biased.

6. The fact that you are asking questions about something sometimes changes the situation for the people concerned and they may change their behaviour.

7. Because a relationship of trust is established interviewees sometimes 'ask questions back', as in Oakley's research. If the interviewer answers these questions this may again change people's behaviour.

■ Using the checklist give examples of how these advantages and disadvantages affected Dobash & Dobash's and Oakley's research.

■ **PROJECT**

Either select a research question from pages 86-89 or write a question of your own that lends itself to the informal interview method of enquiry. Explain why an informal interview is more appropriate than a formal one.

For your chosen area compile and test a small number of open-ended questions.

Method D: Secondary Data

Sociologists often use data which has already been collected to test their hypothesis, rather than conducting their own primary research. Secondary data varies from the highly quantitative statistics to more qualitative personal documents such as diaries or autobiographies. Other types of data which the sociologist might re-analyse include the mass media, historical documents and the research of other sociologists. Research based on secondary data has the practical advantage of being cheap and is often the only way in which a topic can be investigated because of problems associated with primary research.

All secondary sources to a greater or lesser extent suffer from the problem that they have been collected for other purposes, they may not include exactly the information that is needed and they may already have their own biases and inaccuracies. In this chapter we use examples of research based on the media, on statistics and on personal documents to illustrate the uses and limitations of different types of secondary sources.

Statistics

Statistics collected by the government and other organisations are an important source of data for sociologists. Statistics are readily available on a very wide range of social issues including unemployment, crime, family size, divorce, mental illness, industrial action etc. Often it is possible, using these statistics, to compare the experiences of different groups and to find patterns. It is also often possible to look at trends over time.

Some statistics are more useful to the sociologist than others. Some statistics such as those based on the census are more comprehensive than others and clearly not all statistics are equally reliable. The sociologist using statistics in his/her research must discover how concepts have been defined and measured and how this might have changed over time. For example, the crime rate or unemployment rate could change if the way these concepts are defined and measured were to change and this could create a 'false' increase or decrease in crime or unemployment.

Statistics may be used by a sociologist to test an hypothesis, as with Durkheim's research on suicide, or simply to describe patterns in society before developing explanations, as in the example below. Sometimes sociologists, rather than using statistics to describe reality, have studied the statistics themselves and aimed to show how they have been constructed; much of the work within the labelling perspective on deviance has attempted to do this.

Townsend and Davidson: *Inequalities in Health*
Whitehead: *The Health Divide*

Inequalities in Health is based on the report of the working party on inequalities in health set up by the Government in 1977 and chaired by Sir Douglas Black. The aims of the Black Report were:

(i) To assemble available information about the differences in health status among the social classes and about factors which might contribute to these, including relevant data from other industrial countries;

(ii) To analyse this material in order to identify possible causal relationships, to examine the hypotheses that have been formulated and the testing of them, and to assess the implications for policy; and

(iii) To suggest what further research should be initiated.

The Health Divide is essentially an attempt to update the Black Report:

Closely following the format of the original Black Report the review first considers how the experience of health of people living in Britain in the 1980s varies with their occupational class, employment status, gender, area of residence, ethnic origin and housing tenure. It goes on to look at whether the health gap betwen the occupational classes has widened or narrowed in recent years; whether there are differences in the use and availability of health services for different social groups; and whether international comparisons can offer further insight.

What are the advantages of official statistics for studying this particular topic?

Sources of statistics

Both studies are based entirely on secondary data from official statistics and a large number of other studies. Much of the statistical information comes from the Office of Population and Census Surveys (OPCS), a government department in charge of the national census and other surveys and collections of statistics. The main sources are as follows:

Why would these statistics and other statistics based on the census and registration data be regarded as very reliable?

(i) The Registrar General's Decennial Supplements:

The OPCS gathers mortality and morbidity data annually. Every ten years it supplements these annual data with extra information from the ten year census and publishes it as decennial supplements, one on occupational mortality and the other on area mortality.

Since these statistics are based on the census they include all households in Great Britain.

(ii) The OPCS Longitudinal study which has followed vital events for a one per cent sample of the population since 1971.

(iii) The General Household Survey (GHS):

Carried out annually by the Office of Population and Census Surveys. Based on a sample of 15,000 households in the UK, it provides data on a range of topics including health, education, employment, housing and migration. It has been running annually since 1970.

The respondents are asked specific questions on their experiences of chronic and acute sickness and on their use of different aspects of the health service.

Usefulness of statistics

From these sources it is possible to derive information on such factors as occupational class, age, sex, area of residence, ethnic origin, as well as causes of death or experiences of ill health. Townsend and Davidson, and Whitehead, are therefore able to produce a comprehensive picture showing the health chances of different social groups. For example, mortality figures show a sharp class gradient in infant deaths as shown in the graph below (infant deaths are defined as all deaths in children under one year old).

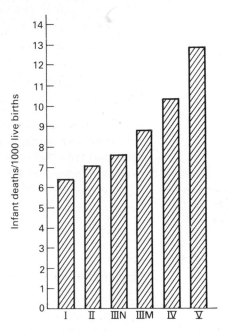

Occupational class of the child's father

■ **These figures are based on the occupational class of the child's father. Why might this be a problem?**

Morbidity figures show that self-reported illness varies according to class and sex, as shown in Table 1.

Table 1: Sickness and medical consultation in early adulthood (average rates per 1,000 population 1971-1976)*

Socio-economic group	Limiting long-standing illness		Restricted activity (in two-week period)		Consultations	
	males	*females*	*males*	*females*	*males*	*females†*
Professional	79	81	78	89	105	134
Managerial	119	115	74	83	113	137
Intermediate	143	140	83	95	116	155
Skilled manual	141	135	87	86	123	147
Semi-skilled manual	168	203	87	102	131	160
Unskilled manual	236	257	101	103	153	158
Ratio unskilled manual to professional	3.0	3.2	1.3	1.2	1.5	1.2

■ **What do these figures suggest is the relationship between ill health and a) class; b) sex?**

* England and Wales for 1971-2.
† 1972-6.

Source: General Household Survey, 1976, HMSO, 1978.

Because the sources which they use are compiled regularly, both studies are also able to look at trends over time, and Whitehead is able to see if patterns have changed since the earlier study. The general conclusion from both studies suggests that although the health chances of the population as a whole are improving, the gap between the classes is growing wider.

Having presented this picture of the social distribution of health chances, both studies go on to develop hypotheses as to the causes of inequalities and to suggest policy changes which could reduce them. However, the quality of any theoretical explanation is partly dependent upon the accuracy of the statistic upon which it is based. Both studies recognise that their statistics are problematic but feel that the overall picture provided is accurate and is supported by a large number of individual studies of smaller areas in Britain, which they quote extensively.

Townsend and Davidson, while using these figures, suggest that there are limitations with them.

Problems with statistics

One of the major problems which they identify is the fact that they must accept the definitions and measurements which have been used in the collection of the statistics rather than defining their concepts themselves. Thus 'health' is defined in terms of mortality and morbidity rather than the preferred measures of 'quality of life' which are used in some of the smaller studies. Class is defined in occupational terms with a married woman's class being recorded in terms of her husband's job regardless of her own occupation.

It is also important to be careful in interpreting statistics. For example, in commenting on the fact that the health chances of the unemployed are poorer than those of the employed, Whitehead states:

> In the face of such abundant evidence of inequality the problems of interpretation need to be borne in mind. Are people who are in poor health more likely to become unemployed, or does the experience of unemployment itself have an adverse effect on health? Is it unemployment or an associated factor which causes areas of high unemployment to have high mortality and morbidity rates? Is the poor health experienced by a nation in times of recession a result solely of unemployment or is it also the result of deteriorating safety standards and increased stress on those in work? Separating the effect of unemployment from these other factors has been difficult.

What hypotheses can be developed about the relationship between class and health?

Similarly there is significant debate over what actually causes the link between occupational class and health chances.

Morbidity figures have further problems.

> There is the disadvantage that rates reflect not only the incidence of disease but also the process by which an individual defines himself (or herself) as ill, seeks medical attention and has his (or her) definition confirmed or legitimated by medical authority. Since we know that there are class-related differences in the propensity of an individual with a given set of symptoms to go for treatment or attention, as well as in the subsequent medical response, we recognize that data of this kind cannot be interpreted clearly.

What factors other than illness influence whether or not people define themselves as sick?

Does this affect your interpretation of the statistics on morbidity rates on page 45?

Both studies show a clear awareness of all these problems and wherever possible the researchers use a wide range of studies to supplement their conclusions on health inequalities. However, some critics still claim that there are no real inequalities in health and that the patterns which are shown are at least partly a result of the way in which the statistics are collected and presented.

■ **QUESTIONS**

1. A sociologist doing research based upon official statistics must accept the way that concepts like health and class or deviance have already been defined and measured. Use examples from this or other studies to show why this might be a problem.

2. What is meant by the claim that statistics are 'social constructs'? To what extent is this true of health statistics?

3. What are the advantages and limitations of statistics for the sociologist? Illustrate using any research examples with which you are familiar.

Mass Media

The mass media may provide our only source of information about a particular event or may be used alongside other sources. Research based on the media usually takes the form of content analysis: this involves identifying key themes or issues and counting up the number of times they occur; or looking at the language and style of a report to discover the impression given.

Using the mass media alone as a source of information does present problems since research shows that the media are not unbiased mirrors of reality. Because of this problem, the media are more often analysed for how they present an event or particular group of people, such as ethnic minorities, women, or the mentally ill, to see how this coverage may then influence public opinion. In this situation the media may become the topic of study rather than simply a source of information. The media may also be analysed to see how the picture of reality given may vary between different newspapers or between television and newspaper coverage, for example.

Glasgow University Media Group: *War and Peace News*

Glasgow University Media Group carried out a number of studies on how the mass media present different aspects of social life. On 1 May 1982 they began video taping all BBC and ITN News bulletins with the aim of analysing coverage of the United Nations Special Session on disarmament which began in June 1982. By coincidence they obtained complete coverage of television news broadcasts of the Falklands War and decided to make this central to their study.

Their main research took the form of a detailed content analysis of television news coverage although they looked at this alongside minutes from meetings, such as those of the BBC News and Current Affairs team and interviews which they conducted in the course of their research. They wanted to identify the main themes of the media coverage of the war and to attempt to explain how these themes developed and how they were to influence public opinion.

Why is it important to gain information from sources other than the media itself?

Carrying out the content analysis

They outlined the three parts of the content analysis:

> Firstly, the indentification of explanatory themes: these are the range of explanations which exist on a specific issue; for example, why the *Belgrano* was sunk. In this instance we list the information and viewpoints available at the time. The second dimension is a quantitative assessment of the appearance of each explanation. Finally we look at how each theme is developed in specific contexts such as in headlines or in news interviews.

Fighting the war

Within the coverage of the fighting, they looked at three major events; the sinking of the Argentine cruiser *Belgrano* on 2 May 1982, the destruction of the British destroyer *Sheffield* on 4 May, and the British attacks on Port Stanley airport on 1 May. They argue that 'the reporting of the destruction of the British destroyer *Sheffield* contrasted sharply with the *Belgrano*.' They identified two key areas; firstly the way the casualties were referred to and secondly the explanation for why each event happened.

(i) *Reporting the casualties*

Casualty statements on the *Belgrano* 3-15 May 1982

	Total	BBC	ITN
Lives lost/loss of life	32	18	14
Lost/loss	16	9	7
Casualties	11	6	5
Missing	6	5	1
Perished	4	2	2
Killing and trapping	3	3	–
Missing presumed dead	3	–	3
Drowning Argentinians	2	–	2
Death toll	2	1	1
Victims	2	–	2
Human disaster	2	2	–
Belgrano disaster	1	–	1
Naval disaster	1	1	–
Missing bodies recovered	1	1	–
Not accounted for	1	1	–
Lost or injured	1	1	–
Sad news	1	1	–
Sad fellow fighting for life	1	–	1
Costing lives	1	–	1
Dwindling hopes	1	–	1
Blood of hundreds of their men	1	–	1
Bottom of the ocean	1	–	1
Grieved over the loss	1	–	1
Funerals when established how many went down	1	1	–

Casualty statements on the *Sheffield*

	Total	BBC	ITN
Casualties	62	45	17
Loss/es/ing	32	12	20
Die	23	13	10
Missing	20	15	5
Dead, missing and wounded	10	2	8
Killed	8	–	8
Dead	7	3	4
Presumed dead and injured/ies	7	4	3
Perished	5	3	2
Lives lost	13	3	10
Killed, missing and wounded	2	2	–
Deaths	2	–	2
Dead and injured	2	2	–
Missing and seriously injured	2	2	–
Seriously injured	2	1	1
Mourning	2	1	1
Death toll	2	1	1
Gave their lives	2	–	2
Grave and tragic	1	–	1
Loss of life	2	1	1
Grave for the men	2	2	–
Agony	1	1	–
British blood spilled	1	1	–
Victims	1	–	1
Fatalities	1	–	1
Sank to her grave	1	–	1
Claimed twenty lives	1	1	–
Tragic loss	1	1	–
Tragic confirmation	1	1	–
Tragic incident	1	1	–
Tragic news	1	1	–
Grim news	1	1	–
Dreadful news	1	1	–
Survived the tragedy	1	1	–
Grave incident	1	1	–
Terrible news	1	1	–

Survival statements on the *Belgrano* 3-15 May 1982

	Total	BBC	ITN
Survivors/survived	77	47	30
Rescued	18	14	4
They/them (survivors)	12	12	–
Picked up	9	6	3
Safe	9	3	6
Saved	7	6	1
Many thought husbands killed	3	3	–
Men alive	3	3	–
(A rescue ship was) lifesaver of 100	3	–	3
Men looked well	2	–	2
Got off/away/in	2	2	–
Many thought husbands dead	1	1	–
Adrift	1	1	–
Could exist easily	1	1	–
Taken to lifeboat	1	1	–
Scores of sailors reunited	1	–	1
All looked well	1	–	1
Came home	1	–	1
Without killing people	1	–	1
Moving with that aim (not killing)	1	–	1

Survival statements on the *Sheffield*

	Total	BBC	ITN
Survived/survivor(s)	31	26	5
Picked up	16	9	7
Safe/saved	13	8	5
Rescued	3	3	–
Crew abandoned ship	3	2	1
Alive	3	3	–
Coming home	2	–	2
Saved themselves	2	2	–
Nearly all accounted for	1	1	–
They get back	1	1	–
Survived the tragedy	1	1	–
Other men transferred	1	1	–
Getting off	1	–	1
Good news	1	–	1
Unhurt	1	–	1

As these tables show, journalists did not use the term 'killed' when referring to those who died on the *Belgrano*.

■ **Using these statistics can you identify the main differences in reporting of casualties from the *Belgrano* and *Sheffield*? Suggest reasons for these differences.**

■ **Content analysis is thought to be a more reliable way of testing an hypothesis or illustrating a point than just using detailed extracts. Why is this so?**

(ii) *Why did each event happen?*

In explaining why the *Belgrano* was sunk, the News coverage concentrated on the fact that it was a 'threat' and that British action was justified despite the fact that the ship was outside the exclusion zone. Again, they provided a detailed list of all accounts which saw the *Belgrano* as a threat as against those which criticised British action. They concluded this analysis:

> Despite the considerable criticism of Britain's action at home and abroad, the predominant theme on the television news was that the sinking was justified. Statements on this outnumber criticisms by well over two to one, and occupy a more dominating position in the coverage. Such statements on the *Belgrano* provided hooks on to which news accounts were hung by journalists and problems debated.
>
> By contrast, statements critical of the British action are rarely pursued.

Explanations for the sinking of the *Sheffield* largely ignored the idea that it might be in retaliation for British action, but rather concentrated on weaknesses in our technology which made us vulnerable. The Glasgow University Media Group argued that these explanations generally fitted in with the interpretation of the war which was being provided by the Ministry of Defence:

> The television news, then, in the main followed a simple military logic. Why had the *Belgrano* been sunk? Answer: because it posed a threat to the Task Force. But when it is asked why *Sheffield* had been sunk, the main answer is because it was incapable of defending itself.

The Home Front

A second theme was how the general public at home were portrayed. Again, they carried out a detailed content analysis, identifying the main themes of the coverage and how they were conveyed. They argued:

> The bulk of TV news reports on the 'Home front' were about the relatives of the Task Force waiting at home. We look at this coverage in detail, finding that the Task Force families – the women in particular – were mainly presented as models of support for the war but were largely denied the possibility of expressing their own opinions and doubts.

The majority of the population had no personal involvement in the war, therefore the experiences of the families of the Task Force were important both in providing a 'human interest' angle to the news and in providing 'surrogate personal involvement' for the rest of us.

From their detailed analysis they argued that the general emphasis was on how supportive and proud the families were.

> We analysed a total of 141 items relating to Task Force families from 390 bulletins recorded over the period 1 May to 14 June 1982. 71 dealt with families waiting at home (23 of these concerned the Royal Navy), 51 with partings and reunions, and 18 with memorial services. In some cases the views of relations were highlighted, as in these reports on the first deaths of British servicemen: 'The father of a Sea Harrier pilot who also died has said, "I'm proud to have a son who died for the country he loved".' (ITN, 13.00, 5.5.82).

What do extracts like these add to the analysis?

When the *Sheffield* sank, one bereaved mother appeared, saying:

> I'm proud of him, I'm extremely proud of him, and if he's gone to war and fought for his country, and died for his country, I'd like everybody to feel that it's not in vain.
> BBC1, 21.00, 6.5.82

But during the whole period of the fighting we found only one case of a bereaved relative's doubts over the campaign being quoted – in this report on the casualties of HMS *Sheffield*:

> 20-year-old Neil Goodall had planned to get engaged at Easter. Instead he sailed with the Task Force . . . His mother who lives in Middlesex said, 'My son never joined the Navy to die for something as wasteful as this.'
> ITN, 22.00, 6.5.82

We found only two interviews with relatives suggesting that the loss of life might not be worth it.

Why might this be important?

Not only did they count up the different types of comments, they also discussed the way in which these were presented or the time of day at which they appeared.

The reporting of the 'war at home' also consistently suggested that those waiting at home were predominantly women. 'In a total of 48 interviews of relatives at home during the period of fighting, only four men appear; three "proud" fathers and Prince Charles who says that Prince Andrew is doing "a most important job".'

All the remaining relatives were wives, mothers and fiancées. Women were also shown in a way which reinforced the conventional female stereotype.

> 'Female relatives are shown without occupation or interests outside the home, waiting anxiously for their men, listening to the news, looking after children and weeping for the dead . . . As well as being shown only with and in relation to their families, women are portrayed not as active members of society, but more as vessels of emotion. T.V. reporters seem scarcely interested in what they think or what they do but only what they feel. There are only two cases in the period when any relatives are invited to speak for themselves about the political implications of the Falklands War.'

Interpreting the data

The Glasgow Media group identified key areas of reporting which they wished to analyse: Fighting the War, the Home Front and Diplomacy (attempts to end the war). For each of these areas they identified patterns in the reporting, such as the emphasis on survivability versus casualties in the reporting of the sinking of the *Belgrano* and *Sheffield*. They supported their findings by reference to detailed statistical analysis and by a fuller discussion of specific reports in terms of language used, placing in news bulletins etc. Through this detailed analysis they provided a picture of how the Falklands War was presented by British television. They also attempted to put this content analysis into an explanatory framework, showing how the reporting of the Falklands War was restricted in three main ways:

1. Those restrictions directly imposed by the Ministry of Defence.
2. Restraints resulting from the lobby system whereby journalists gain information from MPs.
3. The broadcasters' own controls.

They argued two main points:

The Falklands experience revealed conflicts of principle and interest. The right to the free-flow of information in a democratic society was set against the need for censorship in the interests of the war effort. The right to present different points of view about the issue was set against a call to speak for the 'national interest'.

During the Falklands War the general problems of broadcasting independence were sharpened, because keeping public morale on the home front high was seen as part of the war effort, so the 'national interest' demanded that the TV news should paint a picture of national support, and isolate opposition to the war. Too much questioning of the government's policy and the precise interests it served was thought by some to be unpatriotic.

■ QUESTIONS

1. This study suggests that the mass media on their own are an *unreliable* source of secondary data. Can you suggest, using this and other examples, why the mass media might be unreliable?

2. How could a sociologist check the reliability of media accounts?

3. Can you identify any areas of social life where the mass media might provide a central source of secondary data despite problems with reliability?

4. What are the advantages of content analysis as a method for analysing the mass media or personal documents? Are there any disadvantages with this method?

5. Select a current issue or topic such as the representation of women in the media, or the homeless or the unemployed. Carry out your own content analysis study to show how this issue is reported. You must first decide.
    - What media you are going to look at (TV, newspapers etc.).
    - What time period you intend to cover.
    - What are the key themes?

Personal documents

Personal documents (for example diaries, letters, photographs) can be a valuable source of information about current and past events. They provide a fairly accurate record of how a person or group of people thought, felt and looked (in the case of photographs) at a particular time.

Young people's images of attending football: a preliminary analysis of essays by Liverpool school children

The Football Trust-funded Centre for Football Research June 1987

As part of a Liverpool Council-led, anti-hooligan initiative, the Centre for Football Research at Leicester University was involved in helping to draw up a policy document entitled 'Football in the Community'. For this, the researchers undertook a project which aimed at exploring the kinds of images young people have about football in Liverpool. Their sample consisted of children from four Primary schools and 16 Secondary schools. They ranged in age from ten to 16, and came from a variety of religious, ethnic and class backgrounds.

Carrying out the research

Each school was sent an introductory letter, stating clearly that they wanted students to be given free rein to explore their own experiences of football. These could be either real, or their impressions.

Why might this information be valuable?

To ensure that students would write freely, teachers were asked to explain to students that their work would not be marked or graded. These essays were to be anonymous, with students only being asked to state their age, sex and regularity of attendance at matches.

The project produced 1,700 pieces of writing. The researchers write:

> The aim at this stage is to offer the game's administrators, and local club officials, some ideas about the kinds of images young people in a major city like Liverpool have about the sport, particularly in the light of recent tragic events at Bradford and Brussels; to provide schoolteachers with some impressions of the role of football in the lives of young people in Liverpool; to provide background data on the views young people have on crowd behaviour at football; and finally, to examine the potential of material of this kind for use in schools and other institutions as a way of raising the issue of male gang violence at football and elsewhere, for both discussion and policy purposes.

Primary school sample: analysing the data

This produced nearly 180 short written pieces from children between ten and eleven years. The researchers were able to find out both quantitative and qualitative information from these written pieces. For example, they were able to build up some notion of attendance patterns and how this related to gender (Table 2).

Table 2: Patterns of football attendance in four Liverpool primary schools (10-11 years)

Sex	Never attend	Attend regularly/ occasionally	Information not given	Totals
School 1				
Boys	7	23	–	30
Girls	20	5	–	25
School 2				
Boys	3	8	4	15
Girls	11	4	7	22
School 3				
Boys	11	–	–	11
Girls	11	–	–	11
School 4				
Boys	10	24	–	34
Girls	25	5	–	30
Totals	76	91	11	178

What does this information tell us about attendance and gender?

Also by analysing the content of the written pieces they were able to identify common themes and issues. Some of these were:

1. Describing matches – Everton, Liverpool, Manchester United and F.A. Cup Finals.
2. Violence, crowd trouble/fighting and vandalism.
3. Concern about the 'good name' of the city being spoilt by trouble at matches.
4. Many girls considered football 'boring' and too often on TV. 'I hate football because it's boring watching 22 men fighting over a little football just to get it into the net.' (10-year-old girl who never attended football matches.)

Secondary school sample: analysing the data

Here the writers tended to be more experienced and knowledgeable about football. A far greater proportion had actually travelled to away matches to support Liverpool clubs and their writing reflected this broader experience.

From one of the largest comprehensive schools in their sample the researchers were able to draw up information concerning the role spectator violence plays in both male and female accounts of the game (Table 3).

Table 3: An analysis of essays on football from a Liverpool comprehensive school (Age 14-16)

Attendance	Regular		Occasional		Never		
Sex	Boys	Girls	Boys	Girls	Boys	Girls	Totals
Violence as a central theme	28	1	27	9	13	28	106
Violence mentioned but not central	18	5	9	5	2	9	48
Violence dismissed or not mentioned	10	4	6	6	4	12	42
TOTALS	56	10	42	20	19	49	196

As might be expected, themes and issues raised in the secondary school sample tended to be more complex and more deeply explored compared with the primary group. These areas were:

- Positive and negative images of the game
- Experiences of hooliganism
- Images of Merseyside
- Females and football
- Race and racism at football
- It's a great game?
- Manchester United

Here is a small sample of extracts to illustrate the type of writing they received:

Experiences of hooliganism

Female, 15, season ticket holder on the Liverpool Kop

'I have been standing on the Kop for three seasons. Last season, I am proud to say, I never missed a home game. I want to write about two home matches I attended.

At Liverpool v Everton fans were going through the same turnstiles together, sharing a portion of chips. The good-natured humour was all there. Everyone was getting on with everyone else. Absolutely no trouble at all.

But, at Liverpool v Man. Utd. there was no friendship. Just pure hatred. Pure, undiluted hatred. I was in the ground at 2.10 p.m. and what I saw and heard I didn't like. Usually sober and mature men are completely different now. Their faces are twisted with hate and contempt, they are using abusive signs, singing abusive things and sometimes singing a disgusting song about Munich '58 . . . I take pride in my team, my friends who go with me, and they are well-behaved. I normally take pride in how LFC supporters behave, but not this. It is not funny, it's stupid. And both sets of supporters are exactly the same . . . it's frightening.'

Images of Merseyside

Male, 15, regular attender

'The most exciting time I can remember was when Liverpool and Everton went to Wembley together. The atmosphere was terrific . . . The best thing that happened was the happiness and friendliness to the opposing team. All the men went on the train together and the cars were half red and half blue. The women were making rosettes together and we had a party in our street and we all watched the match together.'

Race and racism

Male, 15, occasional attender

What does this tell us about how young people perceive violence at matches?

'The crowd mistook my mate for an Asian boy and they all spat on his head, and kicked him down the steps . . . Then my friend got a match and set fire to the Asian boy's head and said, "Burn, you little brown lump of shit".' By the time we had terrorised a few more Asians, the match had ended. The final score was: four Asians injured, one dead, and no whites injured . . . We are definitely going next week.'

Liverpool supporters standing on the Kop

Females and football

Female, 14, attender

> 'When I went to Anfield Football Club to watch Liverpool and Watford it was a windy day. I was in the front row. I had a good view of the footballers. One man behind me wanted to go to the toilet. He knew if he went he would lose his place. About ten minutes later he just had a "wee" where he was standing, but I complained to my uncle. The bar I was leaning on was wet and it stunk. All the lads just had a wee where they were standing and they didn't feel ashamed. . . Someone in the crowd dropped their ciggy into my jacket and I went home with a ciggy hole in my jacket and rust, and I was glad to go home.'

It's a great game?

Male, 15, all home games

> 'After the game I get some chips. Then, we go home, have a game of football till about 9.30 p.m. Then, we all go in and watch Match of the Day.'

Conclusion

The essays provided a diversity of impressions on the meaning of football to young people in Liverpool. The researchers were left in no doubt about the '. . . cultural centrality of football in a city like Liverpool and the importance attached by young people to the well-being and success of the two local football clubs.'

They argue that much work could be done within schools to reduce the sometimes aggressive rivalry between football clubs, for example, by arranging more sporting links between schools.

On the issue of girls and football they argue that their project throws into 'sharp relief' the interest many girls show about football – clearly many girls want to be 'a fan' irrespective of the sexist comments they often receive on the terraces, and show interest in playing football. Again, schools are seen as potentially very important in helping to break down old rooted traditions of appropriate sports for men and women.

Finally, the essays highlight a degree of racial intolerance. While Liverpool has a sizeable black population, they are not represented on the field or among football supporters. Once again, the researchers argue that schools could play a key role in addressing racially offensive attitudes and behaviour to enable football to become a truly representative sport for the community of Liverpool.

■ QUESTIONS

1. **What is the value of this type of method for collecting information about young people's views on football in Liverpool?**

2. **What type of sociologists would be likely to favour the use of this method?**

2. **What might be the disadvantage of this type of method ?**

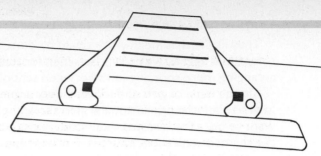

Checklist

ADVANTAGES

1. Most research involving secondary data is cheap, using information which is fairly easily accessible and because time does not have to be spent on primary research, analysis can be relatively quick, so findings are fairly up to date.

2. For some topics of research secondary data is the only way of doing research, for example the use of historical documents by Lasslett and Anderson to look at family structure and social change.

3. Statistics as a form of secondary data can often be used to look at patterns, for example, trends over time (e.g. church attendance), comparisons between countries (e.g. suicide rates) or comparisons between different groups of people (e.g. health chances by social class). (But see disadvantages 1 and 3.)

4. Qualitative data can discover people's meanings and interpretations and can often also be examined systematically to identify patterns by using content analysis.

DISADVANTAGES

1. Research based on pre-existing data must accept the way in which concepts have been defined and measured in the data which is being analysed. For example, research based upon the census must accept its definition of social class. This may not always be the definition which the sociologist would choose.

2. The sources of data may contain biases or inaccuracies which the sociologist cannot check.

3. Quantitative data such as statistics gives no indication of people's meanings, e.g., what do church attendance figures tell us about religious belief?

4. Personal documents are often very subjective, making generalisations difficult. (But see advantage 4.)

5. Some sociologists would argue that no data can be used for analysis without considering the way in which the data was collected.

■ Using the checklist give examples of these points as they apply to different types of secondary data.

■ **PROJECTS**

Choose a question on crime, deviance and social problems (pages 97-99) which you could test using statistics. Would you expect to experience any problems in collecting and interpreting the statistics?

Choose a group of people such as females, males, the unemployed, the police, ethnic minorities. Do a content analysis to show how they are portrayed by the mass media.

Set up an exercise for a group of students to write freely about the same group of people to enable you to discover the public image of your chosen group. How does this compare with the image given by the mass media?

Method E: Using more than one method of research

The studies discussed so far have all been used to illustrate one particular method of research. In reality, many sociologists use more than one method in order to gain different types of data or to test the reliability of their findings from different sources. For example, Humphreys used questionnaires and some unstructured interviews as well as observation; Oakley and Dobash & Dobash asked a number of structured questions as part of their informal interviews and Oakley also used participant observation. Eileen Barker's research on the 'Moonies' illustrates clearly the advantages of using a range of different research methods.

The Reverend Moon presiding over a Unification Church mass wedding

The Making of a Moonie – Choice or Brainwashing?

This book attempts to look at the truth behind the generally held beliefs about the Unification Church (Moonies), to answer questions about Moonie beliefs and to see whether media claims condemning the movement as a 'brainwashing, bizarre sect' are really justified. At the beginning of her research Barker sets herself the following questions:

> . . . why, and in what sorts of circumstances, will what kind of people become Moonies? Why, and in what sorts of circumstances, will what kind of people leave the movement? What is life like in the Unification Church? What kinds of communication system and power structure does the organization have? To what extent, and why, does the movement vary according to time and place? What is the range of the relationships which the Church and its members have with the rest of society? And in what kinds of ways can we best understand and explain the phenomenon of the Unification Church and public reaction to it?

Barker had been interested in researching into the Moonies for some time.

> . . . by now I was becoming fascinated by the Unification Church, and anxious to investigate some of the other reports. In those days, however, the movement was considerably more closed to outsiders than it is today, and it seemed unlikely that I would be able to obtain much more information – unless I were to pretend to become a member myself. This was out of the question for a number of reasons. First, I would have been unhappy about the deception on purely ethical grounds; secondly, I had no desire to give up my job; and thirdly, even if I were to have joined, I would not have been able to go around asking questions on any sort of systematic basis without arousing suspicion.

The opportunity to carry out the study occurred when the Moonies became worried about what was being written about them by people who were relying on the information of ex-members or outsiders, and they offered her access to members themselves.

Being approached by the Moonies had the obvious advantage of guaranteeing their co-operation and Barker was given access to material and people in a way which is unusual for researchers studying religious sects. However, she had to insist that the research could be conducted on her own terms and not controlled by the movement itself. Her study took six years to complete.

To answer her initial questions Barker needed to study the movement at three levels:

1. A personal level – to look at the experiences of individual Moonies.
2. An interpersonal level – to look at the interaction between Moonies and each other and Moonies and non-Moonies.
3. An impersonal level – to look at the structure of the movement, its functions and consequences. To look at the overall role of the movement in society.

To research all of these levels adequately and to check her findings, Barker used several methods of research, as follows:

In-depth interviews

She obtained a complete list of the British membership and interviewed 30 members selected randomly. The average interview lasted between six and eight hours and interviews took place at the centre to which the member

■ Why might covert participant observation be regarded as unethical? How are these ideas different from Humphreys'?

was attached; they were all taped. Barker had an outline of what she wanted to discuss but the order of questions was very flexible. Areas covered included the interviewee's background, why and how they joined the movement, their life in the movement and their understanding of what they were doing.

Participant observation

Barker lived in various centres with the members both at home and abroad over the six-year period of the research. She also attended a variety of workshops and seminars both for existing members and for potential members. The aim of the participant observation was to gain a deeper understanding of the Moonies. Her role as a participant observer went through three distinct stages.

> First there was a passive stage during which I did very little except to watch and listen (doing the washing-up in the kitchen was always a good place for this). Next there was an interactive stage during which I felt familiar enough with the Unification perspective to join in conversations without jarring; Moonies no longer felt they had to 'translate' everything for me, and those Moonies who did not know me would sometimes take me to be a member. Finally there was the active stage. Having learned the social language in the first stage and how to use it in the second, I began in the third stage to explore its range and scope, its potentialities and its limitations. I argued and asked all the awkward questions that I had been afraid to voice too loudly at an earlier stage lest I were not allowed to continue my study. I could no longer be told that I did not understand because, in one sense at least, I patently *did* understand quite a lot – and I was using Unification arguments in my questioning. In this I angered some Moonies and saddened others, but there were those who not only tolerated my probing but actually discussed the problems that they and the movement were facing with an amazing frankness.
>
> Of course, even in the interactive stage it was known that I was not a Moonie. I never pretended that I was, or that I was likely to become one. I admit that I was sometimes evasive, and I certainly did not always say everything that was on my mind, but I cannot remember any occasion on which I consciously lied to a Moonie. Being known to be a non-member had its advantages, but by talking to people who had left the movement I was able to check that I was not missing any of the internal information which was available to rank-and-file members. At the same time, being an outsider who was 'inside' had enormous advantages. I was allowed (even, on certain occasions, expected) to ask questions that no member would have presumed to ask either his leaders or his peers. Furthermore, several Moonies who felt that their problems were not understood by the leaders, and yet would not have dreamed of being disloyal to the movement by talking to their parents or other outsiders, could confide in me because of the very fact that I was both organizationally and emotionally uninvolved. It was not part of my duty to report which individuals were frustrated by the minor niggles of everyday life, or who was unhappily questioning some of the practices of the movement. I just listened. Fears and resentments could be expressed to someone who knew the context, yet would neither judge nor spill the beans. I found, furthermore, that I was the recipient of certain 'classified' information and, even without my asking for it, I was frequently presented with some of the less widely distributed Church literature.

■ **What, for Barker, are the advantages of overt observation?**

There were, however, problems with her role as a participant observer.

> I usually found my time with the movement interesting, and I grew genuinely fond of several individual Moonies, but at no time could I believe in the Unification version of reality. On the other hand, I could not accept the picture

of the movement that outsiders kept telling me I ought to be finding. There was no one with whom I could share, or test, my own picture of reality.

Finally, mention ought to be made of the fact that the people I was studying could be influenced by my presence *because* I was studying them. The observer of the natural world is not nearly as likely as the observer of the social world to influence the data he is studying. It is impossible to know just how much my research 'disturbed' what was happening. There were several occasions on which I mediated between a Moonie and his parents, and I frequently tried to persuade the movement's leaders to see that the members kept in touch with their relations. These interventions, and the giving of information to parents, the media, members of the 'anti-cult movement', and religious and various other officials, I undertook with an awareness that what I was doing could affect the situation. There were also numerous occasions on which my influence was unintended.

One occurred while I was on a twenty-one-day course at which the participants were expected to deliver a lecture. The subject I was allocated was 'The Purpose of the Coming of the Messiah'. I did not exactly enjoy this aspect of my research, but participant observation does involve participation, so I gave the talk, carefully punctuating its delivery with phrases such as 'The *Divine Principle* teaches that . . .' or 'According to the *Principle* . . .'. When I had finished, a member of the audience declared that she had been extremely worried about that particular part of the doctrine, but she now understood it, and she fully accepted that the Reverend Moon was indeed the Messiah. I was horrified. 'But I don't believe it,' I insisted. 'I don't think it's true.' 'Perhaps not,' interrupted the Moonie in charge, 'but God has used Eileen to show Rosemary the truth.'

> **How might an observer attempt to minimise their influence on the situation?**

Questionnaires

Barker recognises the problems of applying a scientific approach in social sciences. However she argues:

> For various reasons, some of which are fairly obvious, the subject matter of the social sciences is considerably less amenable to research than that of the natural sciences. But this does not mean that we cannot improve our knowledge of social patterns, trends and tendencies and gain a more reliable understanding of regularities between variables – of 'what goes with what'. By looking at groups as a whole we can begin to see patterns of relationships, and it becomes easier to detect which occurrences are incidental, even if sensational, and which are 'normal'.

> **What are these 'fairly obvious' reasons? How has this influenced Barker's approach to her research?**

Two years after starting the research she felt that she understood the movement enough to set hypotheses to test on a more systematic basis. The information from formal interviews and participant observation was important in knowing both what questions to ask and how to phrase them. The questionnaire was piloted with 20 members which led to some alterations. The final 41 page questionnaire was given to all English-speaking Moonies in Britain and to some American members. The response rate was very high with only 11 members – after follow-up – failing to reply. Barker gained basic information on these 11 members and argued that they were not significantly different from the respondents. She compared the Moonies with the population of Britain as a whole to compare basic characteristics such as sex, age and social class. She also compared them with a control group matched for age, sex and background and with a group of people who had attended a workshop but not joined the movement. In this way she was able to find out in what ways people who became Moonies differed from other groups in society.

> **What are the advantages of the comparative method to the sociologist?**

Additional information

Barker also gained information from 20 ex-Moonies whom she kept in contact with, from the parents of approximately 100 Moonies, and from anti-cultists and deprogrammers. She also kept a diary of facts and of her own reactions to different situations as a reminder of what happened.

Findings

In her conclusion, Barker comes back to the question 'choice or brainwashing?'. She found no evidence that physical force or other means of affecting biological or physical make-up (e.g. diet) was used on members, although Moonies do make the life and environment of the Unification Church more inviting and cover up bad areas. She argues that the fact that most people 'who are subjected to the Moonies' attempts to recruit them are perfectly capable of refusing to join the movement rules out those explanations which rely totally on Unification techniques of coercion for an explanation of recruitment to the movement.' She suggests that people's background, personalities and past experiences are important in understanding why some people become Moonies and that for these people becoming a Moonie may meet certain personal needs.

■ QUESTION

1. **Barker uses a number of different methods of research. What advantages does this offer the sociologist? Are there any disadvantages?**

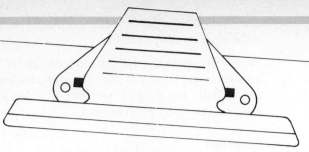

Checklist

ADVANTAGES

1. It is possible to gain both quantitative and qualitative data.

2. It is possible to check the reliability of different sources.

3. It is possible to check that your own interpretation is accurate.

DISADVANTAGES

1. It is both time consuming and costly.

2. Some sociologists would argue that certain methods are unacceptable from their theoretical perspective.

Using the checklist give examples of these points from any of the studies in this section which have used more than one method of research.

PROJECT

Select a question from Section 2 that lends itself to study using several methods of research. Explain how the different methods would complement each other.

Examination questions on sociological method

(Refer to notes on *Writing sociology essays*, page 109)

1. Ethnographic researchers often encounter problems of access to the subject matter of their study, sometimes related to the issue of whether the subject should be conducted overtly or covertly. Compare and contrast the way in which these problems have been dealt with in at least *three* published studies with which you are familiar. (University of London School Examination Board, A/S Level specimen paper June 1988)

2. Compare Official Statistics and Participant Observation as sources of data for sociology. (AEB, 1988)

3. Outline and assess the different ways in which interviews have been used in sociological research. Illustrate your answer with a variety of examples. (AEB, specimen paper, 1989)

4. 'In-depth studies may yield different and sometimes more useful sociological accounts than large-scale studies.' Discuss this statement with reference to studies with which you are familiar. (AEB, 1985)

5. Compare and contrast any two pieces of sociological research with reference to methodological approach, data collection technique, findings and limitations of the studies. (JMB, 1988)

6. You have been asked to carry out a survey of young people's attitudes towards facilities provided on a local authority housing estate. Outline the research issues you would need to consider in carrying the project out. (Oxford, 1987)

Stages in carrying out your research

A sociological enquiry needs to be carefully planned whatever methods you use. The plan below illustrates the main stages which your research may go through.

STAGE 1

Area of interest

This may initially be quite broad such as 'race' or you may have a fairly specific idea in mind such as the experience of ethnic minorities in schools.

STAGE 2

Background research

Reading, talking to people, informal observation, generally collecting ideas and information to tighten up on your area of interest. Keep notes on any background research you do, including all books you refer to.

STAGE 3

Research question or hypothesis

It is useful to have a definite question which you want your research to answer. This can often be stated as an hypothesis – or a general statement of what you expect to find out – which your research can then test. It doesn't matter if your hypothesis is proved wrong. Sometimes, qualitative research might be exploratory and have a much looser framework.

STAGE 4

Choice of research method

This will depend on: (i) your theoretical perspective; (ii) what you are studying; (iii) time/money/access to information or people and other practical considerations. Remember that much research uses more than one method, but it is also important not to be too adventurous.

STAGE 5

Detailed planning of your research

You need to define your concepts quite clearly. For example how are you going to measure 'poverty' or 'class' or 'disruptive

behaviour'? Who can you approach to interview or observe? How will you gain access to the group you want to observe, how will you 'get out' again when the research is finished? Section 1 should have helped you to understand the problems to avoid.

STAGE 6

Pilot study

For surveys you need to test your questions but pilot research can also be useful for qualitative research. A trial observation will help you to pick out important points, practice interviews will make you more confident but would also tell you if your own biases are evident through your tone of voice, facial expressions etc.

STAGE 7

Revise your methods if necessary

You may need to rewrite some of your questions or revise your interviewing style.

STAGE 8

Carry out your research

If you have planned it carefully this is fairly straightforward, but record any problems which you experience.

STAGE 9

Analysis of results

This stage is very important. You must make sure that you relate back to your initial hypothesis or questions and try to reach a conclusion. You may find that your research has raised more questions than it has answered. This is not a problem so long as you describe fully the process you followed and the problems you experienced and possibly make suggestions for future research that is needed.

It is quite useful to keep a research diary in which you record the progress of your research, detailing what you did at each stage, problems you encountered etc. An example of possible diary entries is given on page 84.

This section, through examples, shows how these stages of research may be put into practice. Each chapter takes a central area of the syllabus and suggests a large number of possible research questions which you could use for your own enquiry. One of these questions is then selected, and detailed ideas for planning and carrying out the research are given. The aim of the examples is to show you how different methods can be applied; you should then be able to use the methods in looking at a question or hypothesis of your own. We have tried through the examples to cover most major research methods. If you know what method you intend to use you should go straight to the relevant pages.

Page	Syllabus area	Main method	Other methods
68	Education	Observation	Secondary data for background research
77	Stratification	Social Surveys	Diaries
86	Health, Welfare and Poverty	Informal interviews	Secondary data, observation
97	Crime, Deviance and 'Social Problems'	Media analysis	Informal interviews

Points to consider in choosing your method

In choosing a method of primary research, whatever your hypothesis, there are certain key practical points to consider.

Observation

- Will it be possible to 'get into' a group to observe?
- Will you disturb the natural behaviour?
- How will you record your observations?
- Will you disclose the true purpose of your observation?
- How much time will it take?
- Will the information be representative enough?
- Will you be able to remain objective?

Social Surveys

- Are you going to use a questionnaire or formal interview?
- Are your questions clear and relevant?
- How will you get a representative sample?
- Will your sample be large enough to generalise from?
- Will your information be detailed enough?

Informal Interviews

- How will you get a sample?
- How many people can you interview, will it be enough to be representative?
- Where will the interviews take place?
- How long will the interviews take?
- How will you record the interviews?
- Will your presence influence the answers?
- Can you be sure that you conduct the interviews without bias?
- Is there a difference between what people say and what people do?

Education – Research Questions

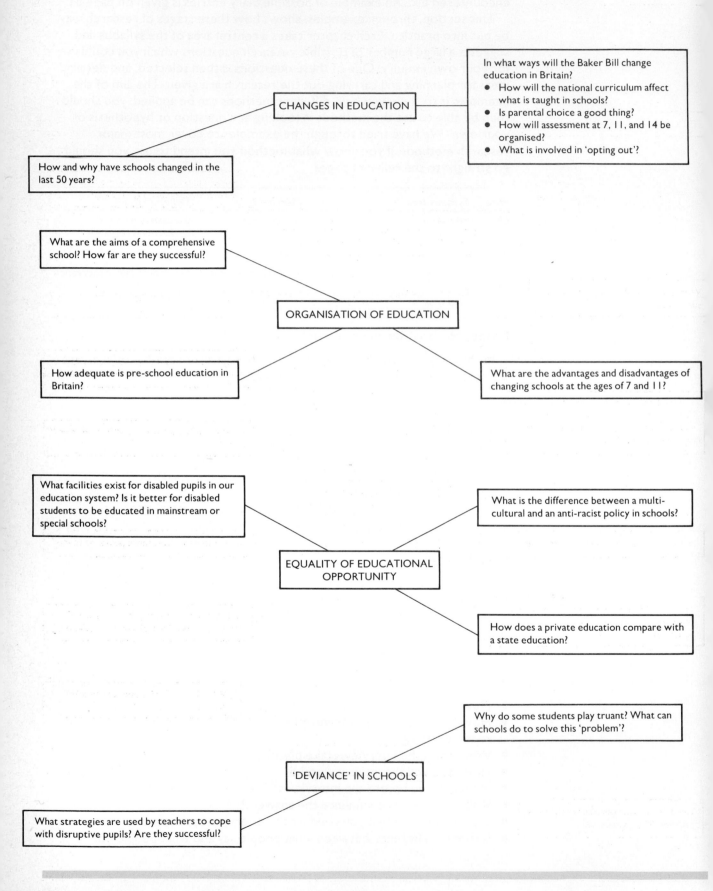

CHANGES IN EDUCATION

In what ways will the Baker Bill change education in Britain?
- How will the national curriculum affect what is taught in schools?
- Is parental choice a good thing?
- How will assessment at 7, 11, and 14 be organised?
- What is involved in 'opting out'?

How and why have schools changed in the last 50 years?

What are the aims of a comprehensive school? How far are they successful?

ORGANISATION OF EDUCATION

How adequate is pre-school education in Britain?

What are the advantages and disadvantages of changing schools at the ages of 7 and 11?

What facilities exist for disabled pupils in our education system? Is it better for disabled students to be educated in mainstream or special schools?

What is the difference between a multi-cultural and an anti-racist policy in schools?

EQUALITY OF EDUCATIONAL OPPORTUNITY

How does a private education compare with a state education?

Why do some students play truant? What can schools do to solve this 'problem'?

'DEVIANCE' IN SCHOOLS

What strategies are used by teachers to cope with disruptive pupils? Are they successful?

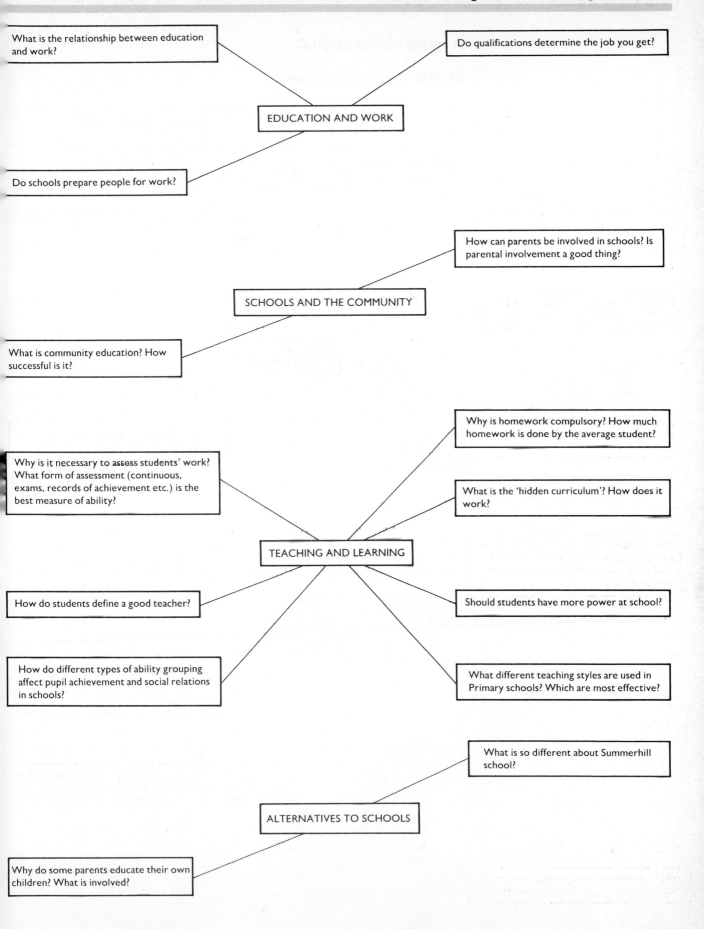

What is the relationship between education and work?

Do qualifications determine the job you get?

EDUCATION AND WORK

Do schools prepare people for work?

How can parents be involved in schools? Is parental involvement a good thing?

SCHOOLS AND THE COMMUNITY

What is community education? How successful is it?

Why is homework compulsory? How much homework is done by the average student?

Why is it necessary to assess students' work? What form of assessment (continuous, exams, records of achievement etc.) is the best measure of ability?

What is the 'hidden curriculum'? How does it work?

TEACHING AND LEARNING

How do students define a good teacher?

Should students have more power at school?

How do different types of ability grouping affect pupil achievement and social relations in schools?

What different teaching styles are used in Primary schools? Which are most effective?

What is so different about Summerhill school?

ALTERNATIVES TO SCHOOLS

Why do some parents educate their own children? What is involved?

A research example

STAGE 1: Area of interest

What strategies are used by teachers to cope with disruptive children? Are they successful?

STAGE 2: Background research

Collect some background information about disruption in schools and how teachers attempt to respond. A good starting place might be your own school/college. *Item A* is an example of how one comprehensive school has drawn up guidelines for teachers on how to respond to problems in the classroom. Has your school/college got something similar? Approach some teachers informally to talk about disruption or refer to other useful sources of information, for example:

- Local Education Authority
- recent reports/research published
- newspaper and magazine articles.

Item B shows extracts taken from *The Guardian* (14.3.89), and attempts to summarise the findings of the Elton Report. The report, carried out by two researchers from Sheffield University's Educational Research Centre, surveyed teachers in England and Wales about their experiences in the classroom. It provides some very useful national statistics and data about disruption and how it is dealt with. From these sources of information make notes on:

- how 'disruption' is being defined;
- what types of incidents occur;
- how teachers attempt to respond to incidents;
- what strategies appear to 'work'.

From this initial groundwork you are now ready to start drawing up an hypothesis.

Item A: Dealing with problem students: A network of support

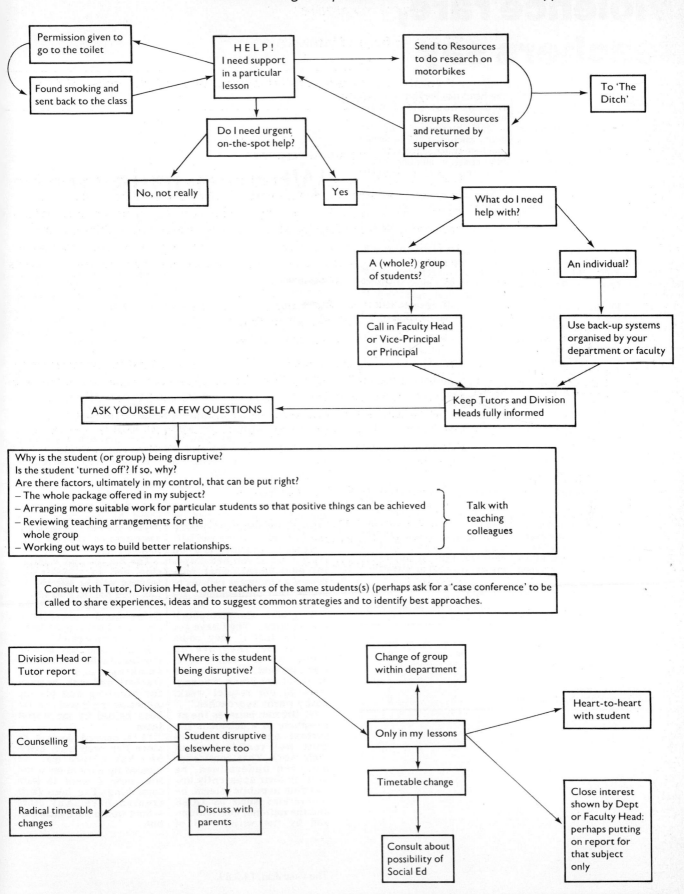

Violence rare, teachers say

Celia Weston

DELIBERATE attacks on teachers by pupils are rare, according to an extensive survey of school discipline published yesterday in the Elton report.

The main problem for most teachers was the wearing effect of constantly dealing with minor misbehaviour which disrupts lessons, the survey found. The majority reported that every day they had to deal with pupils talking out of turn, avoiding work and disrupting lessons.

More than 3,600 primary and secondary teachers completed a questionnaire on pupils' behaviour and the sanctions used to tackle discipline problems. Greater detail was provided through 100 follow-up interviews with staff from 10 inner city comprehensives.

Only about 2 per cent of primary and secondary staff reported that they had been the target of physical aggression in the preceding week. Detailed analysis of questionnaires reporting physical aggression suggested that only about one in 200 teachers were involved in violent incidents.

Aggression did not necessarily involve physical contact, the survey noted. It cited the example of a boy who smashed a teacher's car windscreen with a pick axe handle and threatened the head teacher, but was pacified without blows being exchanged.

Staff interviewed said incidents, such as a girl bringing a machete into school and one boy chasing another with a hammer, were exceptional cases.

The majority of secondary school teachers identified one or two pupils and one or two classes as difficult to deal with. But one in six thought there was a serious discipline problem in their schools.

Primary teachers reported having to deal more frequently with physical aggression between pupils. Seventy four per cent of primary staff dealt with the problem at least once a week (42 per cent secondary) and 17 per cent each day (6 per cent secondary).

Most schools used sanctions such as individual reports, temporary exclusion, detention, withdrawal and long-term or permanent exclusion as the backbone of the school discipline system.

Teachers were investing considerable time, energy and effort to achieve a balanced system of sanctions, incentives and support, the survey found. Priorities to improve discipline identified by teachers were: smaller classes, tougher sanctions against serious misbehaviour, more opportunities to counsel difficult pupils and greater parental involvement

Some of the problems listed in the Elton report

Reported frequency during lessons	At least once a week %	At least daily %
Talking out of turn	97	53
Delaying start of work	87	25
Distracting other pupils	86	26
Physical aggression towards pupils	42	6
Verbal abuse towards teacher	15	1
Damaging objects and furniture	14	1
Physical aggression towards teacher	1.7	0

When pupils are conned not caned

David Ward

CORPORAL punishment was abolished in Lancashire schools in 1983, three years before it was outlawed in state schools in England and Wales.

Brian, a fifth-year pupil at Highfield high school in Blackpool, who has had several brushes with authority, regrets its passing. "I'd prefer to have been caned," he said yesterday. "When you've been caned, that's the end of it. Detention and progress work can go on for ages."

Highfield's headmaster, Mr Derek Digman, has never favoured the big stick, even though he was clouted at school with objects including both a cricket stump and bat.

He said: "Teaching is a con trick. Even if you had corporal punishment, what happens if a youngster refuses to accept that punishment? Do you tie him down?"

He prefers the metaphorical big stick. "They have got to know that if they come against me, they are up against a brick wall." Or at least, he said, that he would bend but not break. "Youngsters do not respect weak, wishy-washy approaches."

Mr Digman believes the atmosphere of a school is important and that teachers must feel confident about their work. That confidence has been undermined, he says, by their apparently low standing in public esteem, by innovations such as GCSE and the national curriculum, and by the withdrawal of their pay negotiating rights.

He and his staff emphasise the importance of good relationships. They give fifth year students some home comforts, including their own base and facilities.

But what happens when pupils fail to respond?

The sanctions begin with detentions, usually linked to some kind of service for the school. "Sometimes there are less meaningful tasks," said Mr Digman. "But we try to ensure that school is not seen as a penal institution."

He says there is no point in responding to truancy with extra school and coercion. Highfield prefers negotiation. Bad behaviour is monitored by a version of the report system and pupils are encouraged towards self-monitoring.

The big sanction is exclusion, and an offender's colleagues will be told why he has been barred from school. After that, they call in the flying squad — one of Lancashire's school support teams to work with a pupil.

Brian, who has been in trouble at school for fighting, smoking, and cheeking teachers and with the police for stealing and playing games on the school roof, has been helped by the support team.

"I've calmed down a lot since I've been here. Everyone has helped me. I've messed up most of my school life, now I want to learn something. I've been fairly treated here. Any other school would have kicked me out."

The Guardian. 14.3.89.

The strategies and sanctions secondary teachers were employing to deal with difficult classes or pupils and their perceived effectiveness

Type of strategy or sanction	Teachers reporting recent use:		Perceived effectiveness (of strategies used)		
	At least once (%)	Often or quite often (%)	Most effective (%)	Most ineffective (%)	
Reasoning with a pupil or pupils in the classroom setting	92	55	21*	12	(of 2281)
Reasoning with a pupil or pupils outside the classroom setting	89	46	32	2	(of 2194)
Requiring a pupil or pupils to do 'extra work' of some sort	76	23	8	10	(of 1871)
Deliberately ignoring minor disuptions or infringements	71	19	3	10	(of 1755)
Keeping a pupil or pupils in (ie detention)	67	17	15	7	(of 1645)
Discussing with the whole class why things are going wrong	66	21	9	10	(of 1626)
Asking a pupil to withdraw temporarily from the room or class	61	11	13	5	(of 1500)
Referring a pupil or pupils to another teacher	50	7	7	4	(of 1237)
Removing privileges	44	9	5	7	(of 1064)
Sending a pupil or pupils direct to the head, deputy or another senior teacher	27	2	14	6	(of 653)
Requesting suspension from school	9	0	9	5	(of 224)

Note: 20% of teachers mentioned some 'other strategy' they had used.

* The figures should be interpreted as follows. Of those teachers (2281 in all) who reported that they had used this particular strategy recently, 21% said it was the 'most effective' strategy they had used whilst 12% said it was the 'most ineffective'.

STAGE 3: Writing an hypothesis

> *Disruption in the classroom is more effectively dealt with by teachers talking and negotiating a solution with a student rather than using punitive strategies.*

In using this hypothesis, terms must be defined. For example, what is meant by 'more effective'? Does it mean more effective in making a student frightened of a teacher or more effective in terms of enabling the student to work in class? You need to make yourself clear.

How will you measure disruption? Start drawing up a checklist of what you will be looking for, i.e.

Forms of student disruption

- bothering other students
- verbal abuse
- moving around the classroom
- not working
- being late to class
- throwing paper

STAGE 4: Choosing your method

Due to the nature of your hypothesis your sample is going to be *teachers*. Attention needs to be given to their gender, age, teaching experience and subject area, because this will ensure a representative sample and also because these variables might correlate with *how* disruption is dealt with. For example, does a teacher's age and gender influence the effectiveness of either negotiation or punishment and if so, why?

STAGE 5: Detailed planning: setting up an observation

Points to consider

As accessibility is not a problem it might be possible to consider either covert or overt observation. If you undertook covert observation in your own normal lessons you would have to consider whether your teachers were a representative sample. However, here we will consider overt observation.

One of the major considerations with this method is what to disclose to the teachers and the pupils. If you explain too honestly you will get great 'performances' from both groups. This has to be avoided if your data is to be valid. You are aiming to record social behaviour as it occurs naturally therefore you must conceal your real objectives. For example: 'My observation is to help gather information about teaching methods in the school.' This raises an important ethical issue, about not telling the truth, which you should consider.

Your location within the classroom is also important. Generally speaking, the more inconspicuous you can be the better. Blend into the background so that your presence does not disturb the normal behaviour of the participants. You are an *observer*, so don't join in with class discussions or activities, which could influence the course of the events you are trying to understand and hence invalidate your data.

Recording data

In some cases it is possible to set up video cameras and/or tape recorders to gain an exact copy of an event or situation. However, this can be very difficult. For example, is the quality of the equipment satisfactory? Should it be concealed to minimise disturbance?

Using a hand-written record sheet like the one below is often a more successful method.

An example of a record sheet for observation

Teacher: .... Age: .... Subject: .... Gender: .... Teaching Experience:		
Forms of Disruption	*Types of response from teacher*	*Effectiveness*
Verbal abuse Bothering other students Not working Being late Throwing things		

'Just act naturally everyone, and. . . action.'

Using this type of record sheet enables you to record information quickly and it *structures* your data so that comparisons between teachers and strategies will be made easier. Be careful not to structure your record sheet too rigidly because this could cause you to miss something important. You should also record the basic layout of the classroom, identifying how students were grouped and how the teacher used the classroom space, i.e. did he/she sit at a desk or move around the classroom? Information concerning the basic content of the lesson (such as what work was set and what the students were expected to do) might also be useful in helping to set the scene when you analyse your data later.

STAGES 6 and 7: Pilot study and revision

A pilot study has two main aims. Firstly, to test the usefulness of your observation sheet and secondly, to enable you to start developing the necessary skills to be a good observer. Visit a couple of classrooms and review your preparation, i.e. are there faults on your observation sheet? How might they be corrected? Does your presence alter behaviour significantly? How might you reduce this? Is classroom observation on its own going to be enough to gauge the effectiveness of different strategies or will you need to follow it up with some interviews? How many observations are necessary to yield meaningful results?

Time spent on experimenting with your method will greatly improve the end result. Remember you are trying to exploit the most positive aspects of your method while suppressing the disadvantages. (See the Checklist, page 17.)

STAGE 8: Carrying out your research

Arrange your observation well in advance so that the students and the teachers know when you plan to observe. Be early so that you can be fully prepared. Arriving late to a lesson and then spending time settling down is a sure way to disrupt the lesson yourself.

Try not to react to any incidents that occur. Nodding, smiling or, even worse, sharing a teacher's disgust about something is disastrous in terms of keeping your objectivity. 'Be cool', stay quiet, and try to remain a detached observer. However, it is very valuable to record anything that occurs that you did not expect and that possibly compromised your position.

STAGE 9: Analysis

Once you have conducted all your observation start analysing your results. Key questions need to be asked, for example:

- Were you able to identify a link between the type of strategy a teacher uses (punitive or negotiative) and its effectiveness on the student?
- Did variables such as age and gender of a teacher correlate with the type of approach taken to deal with disruptions? Why might this be so?
- Were you able to calculate the effectiveness of a strategy in the short term and long term?
- What types of incidents occurred?
- Was your definition of 'disruptive' useful? Did it need revision?
- Were strategies used by the teacher that could not be defined as either punitive or negotiative?

Reflect on some of the information you found out from your background reading, e.g. The Elton Report. How do your findings compare with this report? What are the similarities and the differences?

Finally, while discussing your conclusion, remember also to consider *how* you went about doing your research. What is the value of observation over other methods for this type of research project? What lessons have you learned from using this method? Is there anything you would have liked to improve?

■ **From your knowledge of methods (refer to Section 1 if necessary) are there any criticisms that you would make of this research example? How could you improve it?**

Stratification – *Research Questions*

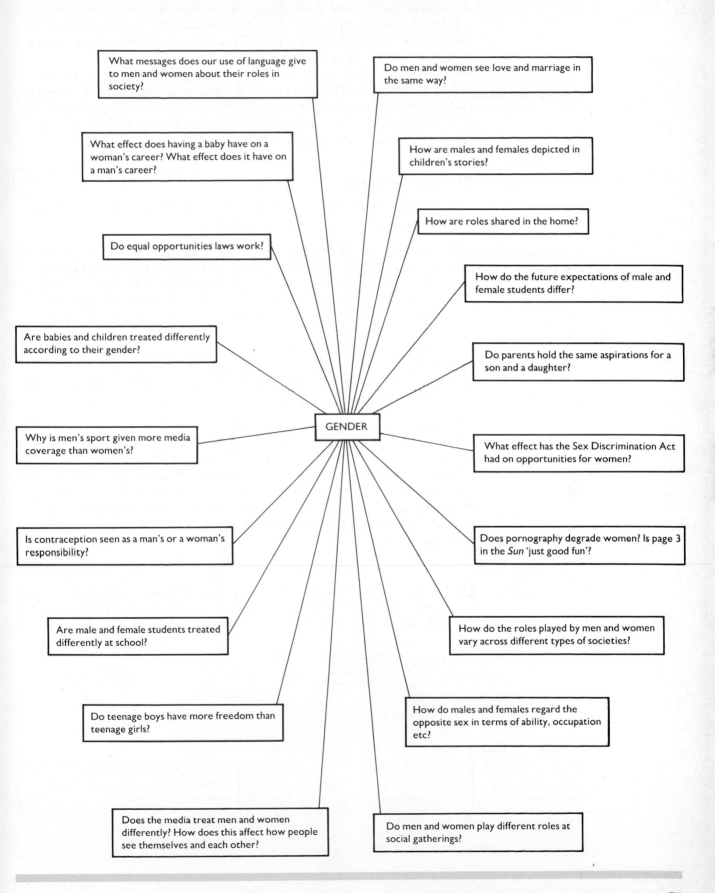

What messages does our use of language give to men and women about their roles in society?

Do men and women see love and marriage in the same way?

What effect does having a baby have on a woman's career? What effect does it have on a man's career?

How are males and females depicted in children's stories?

How are roles shared in the home?

Do equal opportunities laws work?

How do the future expectations of male and female students differ?

Are babies and children treated differently according to their gender?

Do parents hold the same aspirations for a son and a daughter?

GENDER

Why is men's sport given more media coverage than women's?

What effect has the Sex Discrimination Act had on opportunities for women?

Is contraception seen as a man's or a woman's responsibility?

Does pornography degrade women? Is page 3 in the *Sun* 'just good fun'?

Are male and female students treated differently at school?

How do the roles played by men and women vary across different types of societies?

Do teenage boys have more freedom than teenage girls?

How do males and females regard the opposite sex in terms of ability, occupation etc?

Does the media treat men and women differently? How does this affect how people see themselves and each other?

Do men and women play different roles at social gatherings?

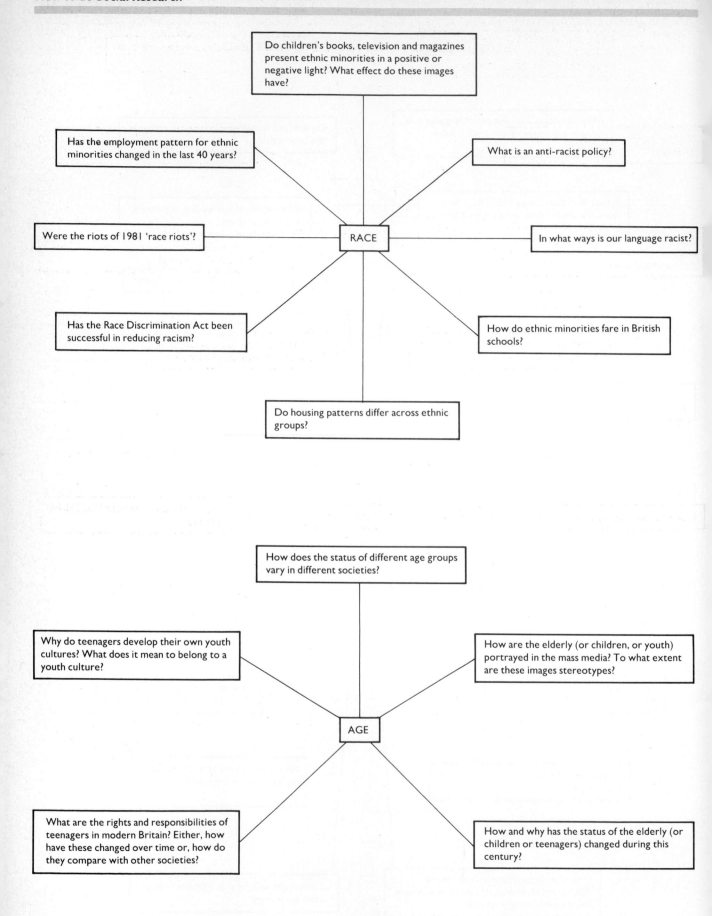

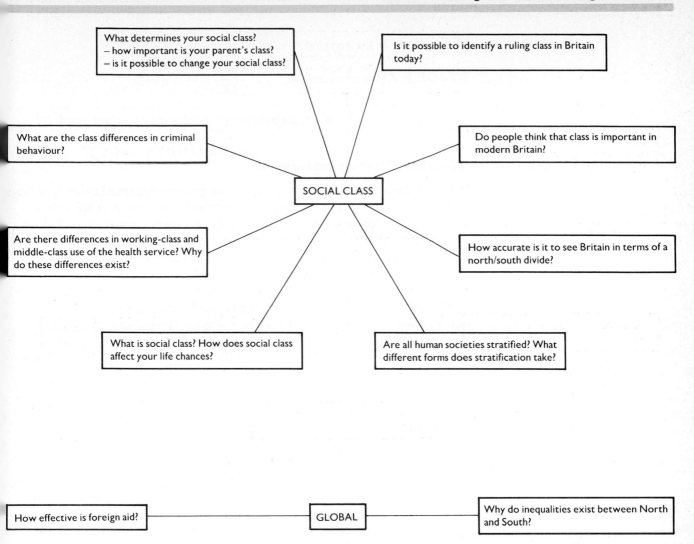

What determines your social class?
– how important is your parent's class?
– is it possible to change your social class?

Is it possible to identify a ruling class in Britain today?

What are the class differences in criminal behaviour?

Do people think that class is important in modern Britain?

SOCIAL CLASS

Are there differences in working-class and middle-class use of the health service? Why do these differences exist?

How accurate is it to see Britain in terms of a north/south divide?

What is social class? How does social class affect your life chances?

Are all human societies stratified? What different forms does stratification take?

How effective is foreign aid?

GLOBAL

Why do inequalities exist between North and South?

A research example

STAGE 1: Area of interest

> *Are babies and children treated differently according to their gender?*

STAGE 2: Background research

Before beginning the research gather some general information on how boys and girls are treated. Just watching children with their parents and other adults in shops, on buses and at home should give you a lot of ideas. Talk to people about the ideas they have about childrearing or their own experiences of childhood. Look at the way male and female children are treated on television programmes or in children's books or comics. An interesting book on this topic is *There's a Good Girl* (Women's Press, 1989) by Marianne Grabrucker, in which the author keeps a diary recording her own and other people's behaviour towards her daughter for the first three years of her life. *Item A* illustrates some of the things she observed. Keep notes on all your background enquiries. From this initial research you will begin to get some ideas for an hypothesis.

Item A

> *11 May 1983 (21 months)*
> I take Anneli to the playground. Two mothers are already there, sitting talking whilst their children play in the sandpit: Stefanie, who's a month older than Anneli, and Erich, who's a month younger. These two children know one another very well and often play together, but they don't know Anneli. Anneli wants to use Erich's spade; he doesn't notice, but the girl comes and takes hold of the spade so Anneli can't have it. I interpret Stefanie's action as a form of defence against a stranger who is intruding on the preserve she and her friend have established. The other two mothers see things differently and say as much, loudly: 'The way Stefanie looks after Erich! He doesn't pay any attention at all, but look how she takes care of his things for him. That's just like a man.' (This man is 20 months old.)
>
> Five minutes later, although neither of them know Anneli at all, they comment on Erich being the cheekiest, although he's the youngest. This is because he's been throwing sand around, common enough in both sexes, I would have thought.
>
> *18 May 1983 (21 months)*
> I have been busy sewing cute little buttons on her jeans, blouses and dresses; they are brightly coloured and depict little animals, fruit, etc. And I can't help but enjoy seeing the sweet little girl in Anneli and wanting to cuddle her. I want her to look nice when we have visitors or when we do something special. In general, I notice I tend to buy bright, cheerful colours for her, often choosing pink, red, turquoise, yellow or light blue. Ellen, on the other hand, says that for her four-year-old son she tends to choose blue, brown, maroon, grey, green, etc. and won't buy anything too fashionable – it has after all got to be suitable for a boy.
>
> *14 June 1983 (22 months)*
> Mothers sit talking while the children play in the play area.
> Four-year-old Hanna is playing on the apparatus with great enthusiasm. She climbs higher and higher, moving with absolute confidence and in no apparent danger. Then her mother rushes across to her, drags her from the climbing

frame, enfolds her in loving, protective arms and says: 'Darling, you could fall off there, it's dangerous to climb so high.' Daughter yells but mother finds an alternative diversion for her in the sand playing with little Anneli. Peace is restored.

We continue our conversation and Hanna's mother now tells me of her five-year-old son's hobbies. 'He loves making things, and sometimes it is dangerous when he's using tools or a knife, but a boy's got to learn to judge this for himself. It's no good just taking the things from him or forbidding him to use them. There is a risk involved, but that's part of being a boy; otherwise he doesn't feel right.'

STAGE 3: Writing an hypothesis

The question as it stands is too broad, so narrow it down to a manageable piece of research. A possible hypothesis is:

> *A child's gender affects the way in which parents respond to children between the ages of two and five, even if the parents are unaware of it.*

This focuses the research on parents rather than all people who are involved with children, and on children between the ages of two and five. Another interesting question is whether male and female parents are equally sexist or non sexist in their attitudes towards children.

STAGE 4: Choosing your method

It would be possible to test this hypothesis using a range of different research methods including participant observation, informal interviews, a social survey or different types of secondary data. Points to consider in choosing a method are outlined on page 67. In this example a social survey provides quantitative information from which to generalise, and is supported with more personal accounts from diaries.

STAGE 5: Detailed planning

Selecting a sample: what sort of people do you want to ask?

Select people who are relevant to the particular hypothesis. For this survey, they must be parents with at least one pre-school child aged two or older.

Because you want to see if the sex of the parent is relevant, try to have equal numbers of male and female respondents. If this is impossible then answers can still be compared using percentages, but it is vital to include *enough* of each sex to make generalisations possible. If people have more than one child in the right age group it is important to make sure that they answer your questions referring only to one.

It would be useful to have equal numbers of male and female children included in your sample.

This may seem unduly complicated, but unless you decide who you want to ask before you do your survey you may find that many of your completed questionnaires are not useful.

For this survey, a *stratified sample* as follows was used:

25 per cent mothers to answer questions on their daughters
25 per cent fathers to answer questions on their daughters
25 per cent mothers to answer questions on their sons
25 per cent fathers to answer questions on their sons.

This should show in general terms whether male and female children are treated differently, but also should show if the sex of the parents affects gender-specific expectations.

How many people to include in the sample?

The sample size needs to be large enough to generalise from but must also be manageable. The sample size must also be large enough to include enough people of each type (males, females etc.) to make comparisons possible. A sample of a hundred people, 25 of each type, would be reasonable.

How to select the actual sample?

There are several possibilities, although all have limitations which must be referred to in your final analysis.

(a) It would be possible to start by asking people who you know and getting them to recommend other people (a 'snowball sample'). This may be practical but obviously is not random in any way.

(b) By selecting (at random or through contacts) groups such as 'mother and toddler' groups and going along and asking people to answer your questions.

(c) By getting lists from health visitors of people in the area with children in the right age range, and contacting them by post or personally. Alternatively you could possibly ask the health visitor to give out your questionnaire for you.

All of these methods would probably only yield mothers and you would have to ask them to take the questionnaire home for fathers to fill in, and then arrange a time to return and collect the completed questionnaires.

(d) A quota sample selected by positioning yourself 'on the street', possibly outside a specialist children's shop, and stopping people who fit your sampling needs.

None of these methods will yield a strictly random sample and it is important that you discuss any limitations in your conclusions; for example, you are less likely to include mothers who return to work when their children are very young if you use (a) or (b).

Using a questionnaire or structured interview

In this case your choice of method will depend on your sampling technique. For all but the quota sample a questionnaire would be most appropriate, since this reduces the amount of travelling which you would have to do. For the quota sample you are more likely to read the questions out and record the answers.

Writing the questions

The most important point is that all questions must be relevant to the hypothesis. This may involve writing a list of questions and then ruthlessly crossing out those which are not important or which simply duplicate other questions. Generally speaking a social survey will obtain a higher response rate if it is brief. Most questions in a social survey will be closed with a number of alternative responses for the respondent to tick. This makes it easier both to complete the survey and to draw up statistics and make comparisons. You may, however, wish to ask a small number of open questions to gain more qualitative data.

Questions must be written carefully so that they are clear and easy to answer. The most common problems which you must avoid are; *double questions* (where there are two parts rather than one and it is impossible to answer each separately; *leading or presuming questions* (these may sometimes reflect your own bias and you need to be aware of this); and *questions which use jargon or vague and unclear language* (these could possibly be interpreted differently by different people).

Talk to parents of small children before writing your questions to give you ideas on important points to cover.

STAGES 6 and 7: Pilot survey and revision

Test your survey by first carrying out a pilot survey. Get a small number of people to fill in your questionnaire *and* comment on it. Ask a couple of the people for whom it is designed, i.e. parents of young children, to fill in the pilot survey. Ask them to be very critical, and ask them if there are any questions:

- which they don't understand;
- where the answer they want to give isn't there;
- which are double or leading;
- which are too personal;
- which they feel are important but which haven't been asked?

From your pilot survey work out how long it will take to complete the main survey. If after the pilot survey, you need to modify or even rewrite your questionnaire, it needs to be re-piloted.

STAGE 8: Carrying out your survey

If you have chosen a quota sample, choose a suitable time (or times) to ask your questions. Consider what time of the day or week is likely to give you the most representative sample group. For any of the other sampling techniques telephone or write in advance to arrange a time to carry out your survey.

Before conducting your survey consider;
(i) Will you tell people exactly what you are studying? It is important to give respondents some explanation but you need to decide whether knowing your hypothesis might influence their answers. In this case it may be sufficient to say that you are studying child-rearing patterns and not mention gender differences.
(ii) How will you collect completed questionnaires (except for the quota sample where this is not a problem) and how will you try to get a high response rate?

STAGE 9: Analysing the results

Once all questionnaires are returned, sort them for analysis. Record all your answers either on a computer or manually on paper. This allows you to count up responses and to look for patterns. It is important to analyse results with the initial hypothesis in mind.

Concluding your survey

To what extent can the hypothesis be supported? What problems did you experience? How might these have influenced the results?

Additional ideas for research

The survey will have provided mostly statistical data, which could be supplemented by gaining more detailed descriptive accounts by asking a smaller number of people to record their experiences with their child in the form of a diary. Refer back to the extracts from Marianne Grabrucker's diary on pages 80-81 to see the type of data which you might hope to get from a diary.

If you use diaries as a method of research it is important to consider:

- what exactly you want to find out and what guidance you will give to parents to help them complete their diaries;
- how many diaries you need, and how you will select people to fill them in;
- how typical of parents are your respondents likely to be?

Therefore, what use can you make of your results?

Final conclusions

In what ways did the data provided from each source differ? Using all available data, is the hypothesis supported or not? What further research, if any, do you think is needed?

Extracts from research diary

10.9.90	Since we talked about gender in Sociology, I keep noticing how boys and girls behave differently and are treated differently. I'd like to find out when this different treatment starts so I've decided to do my enquiry on the way parents treat small children of different sexes.
17.9.90	Spent the weekend with my sister who has three-year-old twins, Tony and Mary. I tried to observe all of the ways in which they were treated differently and ways in which they were treated the same. I noticed a difference in clothes and the way Mary was expected to be neater and cleaner when eating, for example. There were also subtle differences like the tone of voice used to praise them and tell them off. There was no difference in the type of games they played or in their favourite toys, though, this surprised me. I think I'll concentrate my research on toys, clothes, discipline, types of play and

expectations about cleanliness, tidiness etc.

24.9.90 Spent ages in the library trying to find some books and articles on childrearing patterns. There's very little recent research. Talked to Mrs. Jones about my hypothesis, she says it would be too difficult and I need to look at a more concentrated age group rather than just young children. She also suggested I should look at how attitudes of mothers and fathers differ.

1.10.90 Decided to use a questionnaire as my main method as I want to see if there are any general patterns. I'd like to find a way of backing this up with more personal and detailed information though. Wrote out some questions.

9.10.90 I asked my sister and her husband to fill in my questionnaire and to talk to me about the questions. It's hard not to word questions in a way which doesn't give away what I'm trying to find out. I don't want to do this because most people don't like to think that they are sexist and might 'fix' their answers. I need to rewrite a few questions. They also pointed out some other questions I could ask.

23.10.90 Spent the last two weeks revising my questionnaire. Contacted the manager of Mothercare to see if I can stand outside and hand out my questionnaire.

3.11.90 Stood outside Mothercare for two hours this morning handing out questionnaires. Very few people refused. I thought that a Saturday would be best if I wanted to get men as well as women, but I'll still need to go into town again to get some more men. Perhaps I should go to a different shop to get a less biased sample.

■ **From your knowledge of methods (refer to Section 1 if necessary) are there any criticisms that you would make of this research example? How could you improve it?**

Health Welfare and Poverty – Research Questions

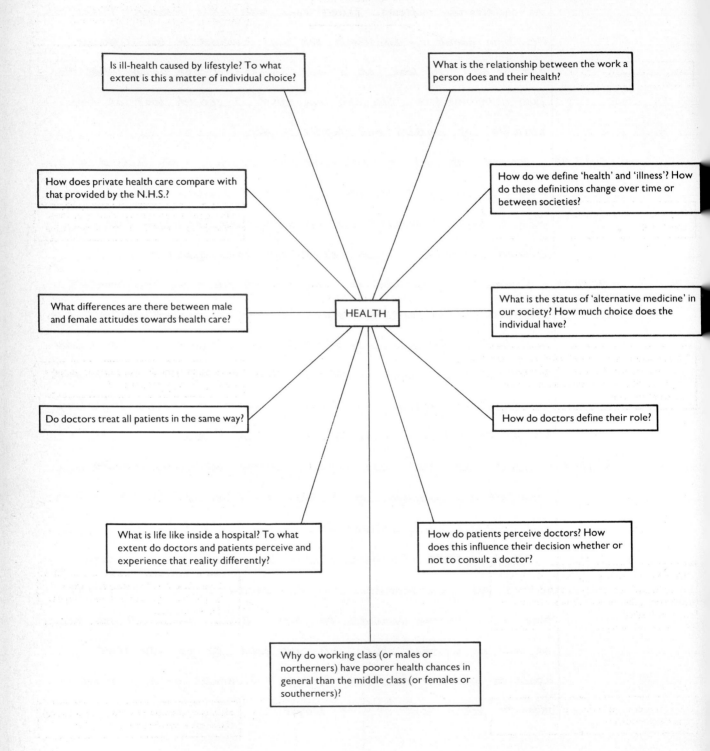

Is ill-health caused by lifestyle? To what extent is this a matter of individual choice?

What is the relationship between the work a person does and their health?

How does private health care compare with that provided by the N.H.S.?

How do we define 'health' and 'illness'? How do these definitions change over time or between societies?

What differences are there between male and female attitudes towards health care?

HEALTH

What is the status of 'alternative medicine' in our society? How much choice does the individual have?

Do doctors treat all patients in the same way?

How do doctors define their role?

What is life like inside a hospital? To what extent do doctors and patients perceive and experience that reality differently?

How do patients perceive doctors? How does this influence their decision whether or not to consult a doctor?

Why do working class (or males or northerners) have poorer health chances in general than the middle class (or females or southerners)?

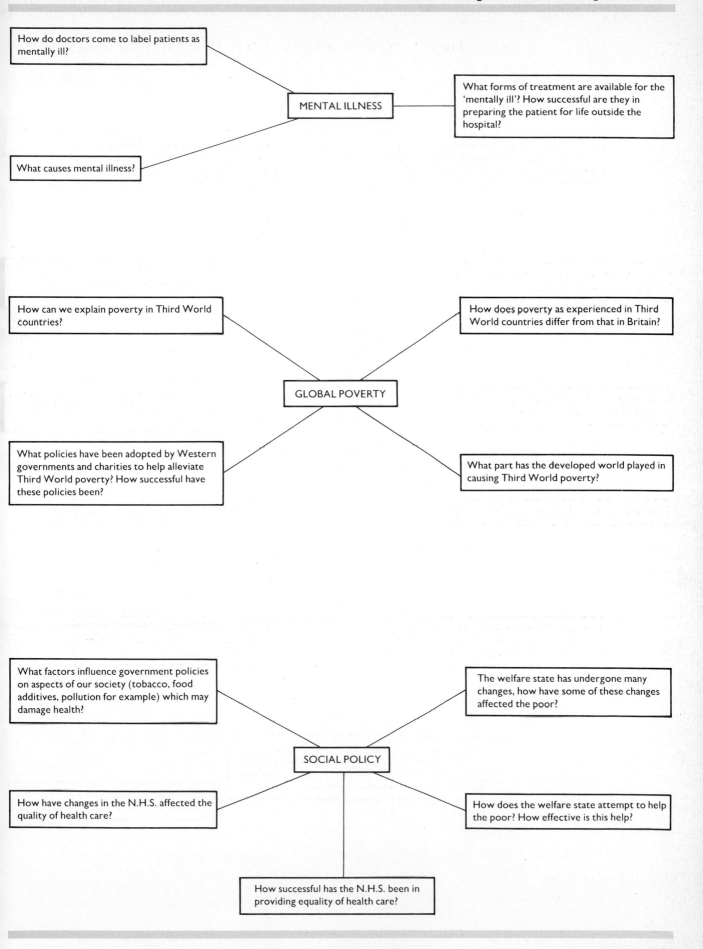

How do doctors come to label patients as mentally ill?

What forms of treatment are available for the 'mentally ill'? How successful are they in preparing the patient for life outside the hospital?

MENTAL ILLNESS

What causes mental illness?

How can we explain poverty in Third World countries?

How does poverty as experienced in Third World countries differ from that in Britain?

GLOBAL POVERTY

What policies have been adopted by Western governments and charities to help alleviate Third World poverty? How successful have these policies been?

What part has the developed world played in causing Third World poverty?

What factors influence government policies on aspects of our society (tobacco, food additives, pollution for example) which may damage health?

The welfare state has undergone many changes, how have some of these changes affected the poor?

SOCIAL POLICY

How have changes in the N.H.S. affected the quality of health care?

How does the welfare state attempt to help the poor? How effective is this help?

How successful has the N.H.S. been in providing equality of health care?

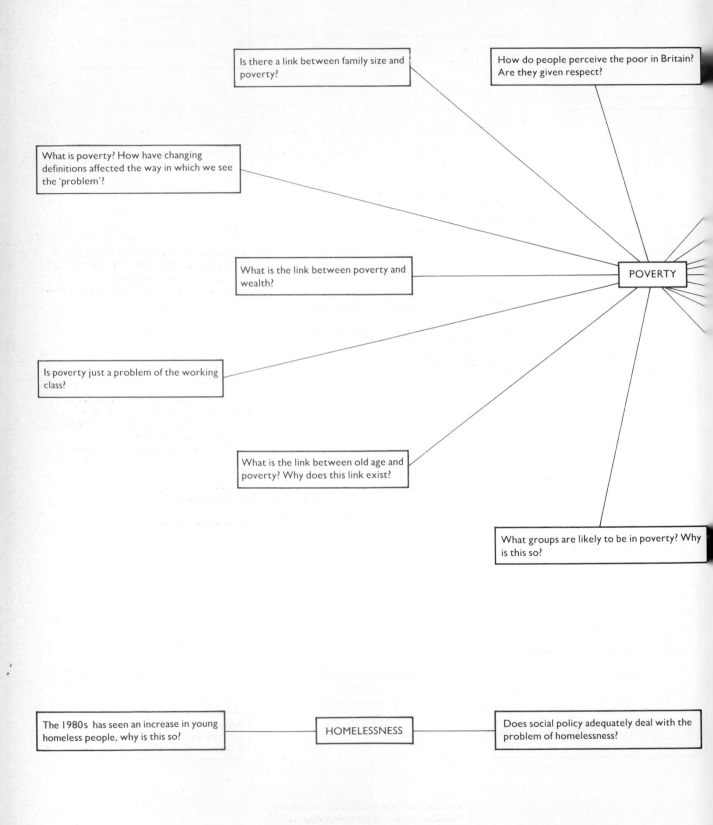

Is there a link between family size and poverty?

How do people perceive the poor in Britain? Are they given respect?

What is poverty? How have changing definitions affected the way in which we see the 'problem'?

What is the link between poverty and wealth?

POVERTY

Is poverty just a problem of the working class?

What is the link between old age and poverty? Why does this link exist?

What groups are likely to be in poverty? Why is this so?

The 1980s has seen an increase in young homeless people, why is this so?

HOMELESSNESS

Does social policy adequately deal with the problem of homelessness?

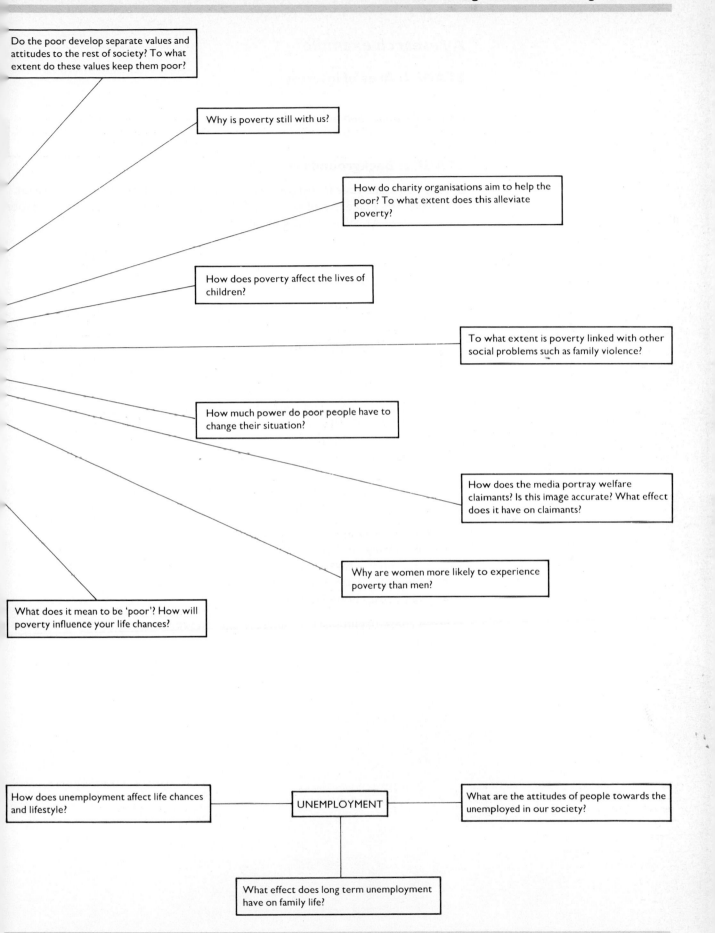

Do the poor develop separate values and attitudes to the rest of society? To what extent do these values keep them poor?

Why is poverty still with us?

How do charity organisations aim to help the poor? To what extent does this alleviate poverty?

How does poverty affect the lives of children?

To what extent is poverty linked with other social problems such as family violence?

How much power do poor people have to change their situation?

How does the media portray welfare claimants? Is this image accurate? What effect does it have on claimants?

Why are women more likely to experience poverty than men?

What does it mean to be 'poor'? How will poverty influence your life chances?

How does unemployment affect life chances and lifestyle?

UNEMPLOYMENT

What are the attitudes of people towards the unemployed in our society?

What effect does long term unemployment have on family life?

A research example

STAGE 1: Area of interest

> *The 1980s has seen an increase in young homeless people. Why is this?*

STAGE 2: Background research

Before you start your investigation gather some general information about homelessness. Make use of relevant TV documentaries, magazine/newspaper articles (*Item A*). Write to organisations such as:

1. Shelter
   88 Old Street
   London EC1 9HV.

2. Local Housing Department.

3. Local D.H.S.S. Office.

4. Local Charity/Voluntary Agencies.

Personal Documents: Item B

Shelter has recently been involved in a special research project inviting young homeless people to keep a 30-day diary of their experiences on the streets. Diarists were promised a £5 postal order if they returned a completed diary. Diaries were given out from day centres and night shelters throughout Britain. More than a hundred completed diaries were returned and they make illuminating reading about the despair and loneliness these young people face.

All these secondary sources will help you to build a very general picture of homelessness. Try to find out:

- who the young homeless are;
- if/how they have changed in 1980s;
- what the law says about homelessness;
- what organisations exist to help the homeless;
- what *causes* homelessness.

From these preliminary enquiries begin to identify specific issues or areas of interest.

Item A

Waterloo homeless beg for change at the end of the line

Madelaine Bunting

BEGGING in Waterloo Station, London, is a growth industry. It may not be as lucrative as other patches, but you can usually pick up between £5 and £15 in a few hours. Besides, Waterloo is within spitting distance of the Bullring, or cardboard city, where about 200 homeless spend the night under Waterloo Bridge.

Sandy, aged 18, said she once earned £85 in a day in Leicester Square. The general rule of thumb is that girls earn more than boys, and children earn more than the adults. The thinner, and the smaller you are, the more likely you are to pluck the heart-strings of old ladies.

Unless Sandy needs a new sleeping-bag or is feeling particularly hungry, she sticks to Waterloo where she can be more certain of a quiet day's work with fewer police and fewer other beggars.

The first complaint is the police. "We're not doing any harm, we're not mugging anyone or snatching handbags. I can't see why the police give us so much hassle," argued a gentle 17-year-old boy called Mark. "We're always polite when we beg and always say excuse me."

Relations between the homeless and police appear a well-worn and fairly amicable routine of warnings, cautions and the occasional arrest. Although police policy is to arrest those caught begging, as Inspector Berryman of Waterloo's transport police admitted, in practice he simply does not have the manpower. Arrests usually mean a day in jail and a fine. When Mark was fined £25, he worked overtime begging for a couple of days to pay it off.

"Little Hammie" says she has been on the streets since she was eight; she has been arrested so many times she has lost count. "Everyone knows Little Hammie — the police, the traders, the newspaper man," she said proudly.

Love affairs wax and wane, but dogs command the most loyal affection. Mark sets aside £2 a day to feed his dog and Sandy will happily go without so long as her dog is fed.

No hostel will accept dogs, and Mark and Sandy passionately declare they would rather die than be parted from their dogs.

Media attention is welcomed; an interview is happily exchanged for a chocolate eclair. There follows a cheerfully delivered tale of a broken home, beatings from step-parents, mental hospitals, hostels and jail, which ends with the familiar line: "I can't get anywhere to live because I haven't any money, and I can't get a job because I haven't got an address."

Most have tried various hostels or missions, but there are long waiting lists for accommodation. Couples don't want to be split up in single sex hostels. Besides, as "Blogwin" put it, waving her arms expansively in the air: "I love my freedom."

Source: *The Guardian* 17.8.1989

Growing army of beggars in London

Stephen Cook

ON A GREY morning with seagulls swooping over the Thames, Barry and his dog Tripper have secured a prime begging pitch — one end of Hungerford Bridge, the central London pedestrian link between north and south banks. Commuters hurry past, dropping occasional coins in his black woollen hat.

"It's the ones who don't even look at you who make me feel angry," says Barry, a 27-year-old from Bradford with a blond beard, an earring, and sharp blue eyes. "They just blank you out. They don't have to give, but at least they could look at you and see that you're another human being.

"Some of them say things to you, like why don't you get a job, and some get pretty abusive. But what can you say back? It's degrading enough having to beg in the first place. The best givers are the poorer-looking ones — perhaps they know what it's like."

Barry is part of a growing army of beggars in the streets of the capital. Five years ago it was unusual to be accosted and asked for money on a walk round the centre, but now it is almost inevitable, and the supplicants are younger.

Barry arrived seven years ago, worked in kitchens and lived in a squat. When Southwark council reclaimed the squat, he lived in bed-and-breakfast hotels; when the April change in social security made that impossible, he moved to the "bull ring" — the walkways under Waterloo Bridge roundabout where 50 people or more sleep.

He says he gets £16 a fortnight from the Department of Social Security, and the last three days' begging has brought him £11. "The problem with work is there's a job for every 10 men and if you're homeless they don't want to know."

Half way across the bridge stands David Tripp, aged 43, tunelessly playing a mouth organ. He has spent half his life in mental hospitals and prison and now lives in a supported housing scheme in Lewisham.

He has £32 a week left after rent and says he begs to pass the time.

Twenty yards further on stands Stephen, whose ingeniously self-made coat and plastic shoes deserve a place in the Tate Gallery. He is a cheerful, grimy 37-year-old Rhodesian who swigs from a beer can.

He gets £33 a week social security, sleeps in Bedford Square or Russell Square, and reckons to make £5 from a good day's begging. "I used to line up to work at Claridge's, in the kitchens, but there are too many in the queue now. Besides, I'm rich now — I've got a radio."

Source: *The Guardian* 12.11.1988

Item B: Shelter Diaries: Young homeless people write about their lives

A 16-year-old woman from Sevenoaks has been in London 3 months.

Day 1   £0
Today I stayed up the Embankment. I can't sign on because I'm 16. I have to go on YTS, but I'm homeless, so I can't.

Day 2   £3
Went begging today, bought a cheeseburger and some fags. Stayed in car park at Euston Station.

Day 3   £0
Got arrested early hours of this morning for being abusive to a copper. Wow! Got out of the cells 3 hours later.

Day 4   £15
Met a reporter today who gave me £15 for giving her a story on homelessness. Wow! Bought a pizza.

Day 5   £5
Still got £5 from yesterday and bought some chips. Still staying in Euston but having hassle from pigs. Might have to move up Embankment tomorrow.

Day 6   £0
What a bad day. Got smacked in gob by drunk yuppie, spent all night in hospital, St Thomas's.

Day 7   £0
Got a fat lip. Can't eat as mouth hurts.

Day 8   £0
Lip a bit better. Ate some chips again. Still up Embankment.

Day 9   £6
Begged up £6. Ate sausage, beans and chips. Got no sleep up Embankment, a Shaggy went mad and kept us awake all night.

Day 10   £1
Fed up today. Had enough.

Day 11   £0
I want to go home. Mum won't have me. Embankment.

Day 12   £3
No money, got a cold.

Day 13   £2
Feel ill today.

Day 14   £1
Got bad cough as well. Lost my voice. The squat got busted last night and the pigs have evicted us.

Day 22
Slept up Temple last night, quite warm.

Day 23
Went back to squat to see if we can get back in, but the bastards have padlocked it.

Day 24
Felt really ill today, don't know what's wrong. Went to doctor, he said I need to find a home.

Day 25   £1
Went to Soho Project, they might be able to get me into Bina Gardens. Ate chips.

Day 26   £5
Got my interview with Bina tomorrow, wow, hope I get in. Begged £5. Ate Wimpy.

Day 27   £3
Interview with Bina OK. Move in tomorrow. At last. Ate more chips.

Day 28   £0
Moved into Bina, it's OK. People friendly, a bed at last, I can't believe it. Ate loads.

Day 29   £0
Slept in today, it was great. Washed clothes.

Day 30
Starting YTS next week, child care. Can get some dosh now, things are looking up. Bye.

A 19-year-old man, who has been in London for one week, is homeless 'especially because the DHSS don't help you and my father is an alcoholic'.

Day 1   £1.55
Centrepoint. It's overcrowded. They don't, the DHSS I mean, they don't give you the help you need or advice or anything. I was just walking around *all day*. £1.55 and it's not enough.

Day 2   £1.55
Walked around town all day. There was nothing open but some cafes until about 10am. Went to Buckingham Palace. Slept at a night shelter.

Day 3   £1.55
Today is a very boring Sunday. Nothing to do so I just walked around.

Day 4   £1.55
Today I went to Alone in London to try to get a place to live. But no vacancies, nowhere available. Went to the Job Centre looking for work, got an interview but the job was taken.

Day 5   £1.55
Went to Alone in London. No vacancies today neither. No work. Bored myself to death by just walking around for 9 hours. Went back to hostel.

Day 6   £1.55
Went to Alone in London. No vacancies were available AGAIN. Tried to get a Bed and Breakfast, but couldn't get in cos I couldn't pay the rent. So I went to the DHSS but they say I can't have it, cos I've got no address.

Day 7   £1.55
Went to Alone in London, no vacancies again. Went to Job Centres, got interviews but I didn't have no qualifications or anything. Went to St James's Park and got really pissed off, cos the police hassled me all day.

Day 8   £1.55
Went to Alone in London. Same shit. Felt really pissed off. Walked around all day, nothing else to do but look at girls.

Day 9   £1.55
Today is Saturday so there is nothing I can do to sort myself out, so I went walking all day.

Day 10   £1.55
Met some friends, went around with them. Felt sick, had fever and headache and quite pissed off.

STAGE 3: Writing an hypothesis

Now focus on one particular aspect of homelessness. Bear in mind issues of time, manageability, access to information etc. A possible hypothesis is:

> *The increase in the number of homeless young people in my local area during the 1980s is largely the result of changes in Government policies.*

This statement narrows down the field of study to *the young* in a *local area*, and to *one particular cause* of homelessness. The aim of the research will be to either prove or disprove this statement.

Using this hypothesis immediately presents three key issues for investigation. These are:

A   To identify who the young homeless are in the local area.
B   To discover if/how the number of young homeless has changed.
C   To find out about recent Government policies that relate to the young homeless.

Your research *methods* will therefore be partly shaped by the attempt to discuss these issues.

STAGE 4: Choosing your method

Attempting to gather a local sample of homeless young people could be very difficult indeed, because

- How would you contact them?
- How could you make sure your sample was 'representative' of the area?
- How would you set up interviews/surveys?

It might be easier to have a sample drawn from agencies who work closely with the young homeless. Professional and voluntary organisations in your area should be able to provide a reasonably accurate picture of homelessness.

STAGE 5: Detailed planning

Taking a method of enquiry and turning it into research

It is possible to take *two* methods of enquiry to help investigate your hypothesis. For example, you could take observations and informal interviews. Personal observation while working at a Night Shelter or Advice Centre could provide a valuable glimpse at the day-to-day reality of being young and homeless. From this it might be possible to build up some individual profiles of the circumstances that have led some people into homelessness. Much will depend upon the length of time spent and the quality of the relationships that you build up. Obviously confidentiality and sensitivity is crucial and you have to consider whether you should disclose your true purpose.

The information gained from this method would provide a very useful link between your background reading (e.g. The Shelter Diaries) and the information obtained from professional and voluntary workers through informal interviews.

Informal interviews – points to consider

(i) *Setting up the interview*

In setting up an informal interview consider whether it is wise to tell your interviewee/s what your hypothesis is. Would this influence a respondent's decision to take part in your research? Might it influence their response to your questions? Usually, in the interests of reducing bias, it is better to disclose only a very general purpose of your research, eg seeking to learn about homelessness in your local area. **Remember that your sample will not be random because you will probably only be contacting available local people**. Some thought also needs to go into where the interviews will take place. Is it possible for them to occur in the same place? This would help standardise the setting. Or will it involve you travelling to their territory – either a work-place or home? Familiar surroundings will probably increase the interviewees' confidence and therefore help to yield more information. However, you would have to be adaptable and capable of handling the interview, whatever the setting. Ideally the location must be quiet and comfortable. Try to ensure that the respondent can give you their full attention for the duration of the interview, without interruption.

(ii) *Organising questions*

To start your interview use some general questions that aim to ease both you and your interviewee into the interview. For example:

- What is the full title of your job?
- How long have you been working in this post?
- What does the post involve?

The main part of your interview should consist of more specific areas for discussion that directly relate to your hypothesis. For example, 'What would you say are the main causes of homelessness among the young?' All questions must be set up in such a way as to give the interviewees maximum opportunity to express their attitudes and opinions. Ensure that your attitudes and opinions are kept *out* of the interview. Be ready to probe further on any point that is raised. Follow up on any issue that you might have ignored, but that the interviewee identifies as important. The crucial factor is to be a *good listener*. Tune into the respondent's wavelength and try not to get too bogged down worrying about what your next question will be. Look interested, nod, smile, encourage your respondent to *talk*.

All these things can be more easily achieved if you are not scribbling down answers. A tape recorder, set up inconspicuously, can really help you to concentrate on developing a friendly, relaxed atmosphere that invites discussion. Remember a good interview is one where the interviewee does most or all of the talking.

STAGES 6 and 7: Pilot study and revision

There is no doubt that a good informal interview technique has to be practised! Using pseudo-interviewees, experiment with the questions you have set up. Are they clear? Do they invite discussion or just one word answers? Experiment with your own presentation and style. Are you relaxed? Do you look interested? Develop skills on how to probe for further information. Consider how you will finish your interview. Will you provide an opportunity for the interviewee to add a last comment about the topic under discussion? This could be a useful way of securing any hitherto unexpressed thoughts and opinions. At the very least you should always remember to thank your interviewee for taking part.

From these practice run-throughs be willing to re-think how to set up your interview/s. Be adaptable and *learn* from your mistakes. The quality of the final interview greatly depends upon the energy and enthusiasm you put into the preparation for it.

STAGE 8: Carrying out your research

Being well organised is important. If you are using a tape recorder, have a sound check to set the correct recording levels. Bring a spare tape in case of any problems. Are your questions clearly written down on an interview schedule sheet? Is the interview room comfortable? Are there easy chairs to promote a more relaxed atmosphere? Have you allowed plenty of *time* so that the interviews will not be rushed? All your hard preparation could be spoiled if you don't pay attention to final details.

STAGE 9: Analysis of results

Once your interviews have taken place and the results have been recorded, analyse your findings. The greatest advantage of taped interviews over hand-written recordings is that *nothing* is lost; they provide a pure representation of what was said during the interview. Your task is to extract key points that relate to your hypothesis, ie

- What have your interviewees told you about homelessness and the young?

- What are the Government's policies on homelessness?
- Is homelessness related to these policies?
- In what ways is it related?

Weigh up the extent to which your hypothesis is supported or disproved. If you conducted an observation at a hostel how has this contributed to an understanding of the *causes* of homelessness? How does this link with the information gained from the interviews? Reflect on *how* you conducted your research. What were the advantages of your method/s? What problems did you experience, and how did you attempt to overcome them? Would you do anything differently a second time? Has your research raised more questions than it has answered? If so, this is not necessarily a problem. The *process* you have worked through is as, or more, important than the results you found.

◼ **From your knowledge of methods (refer to Section I if necessary) are there any criticisms that you would make of this research example? How could you improve it?**

Crime Deviance and 'Social Problems' – Research Questions

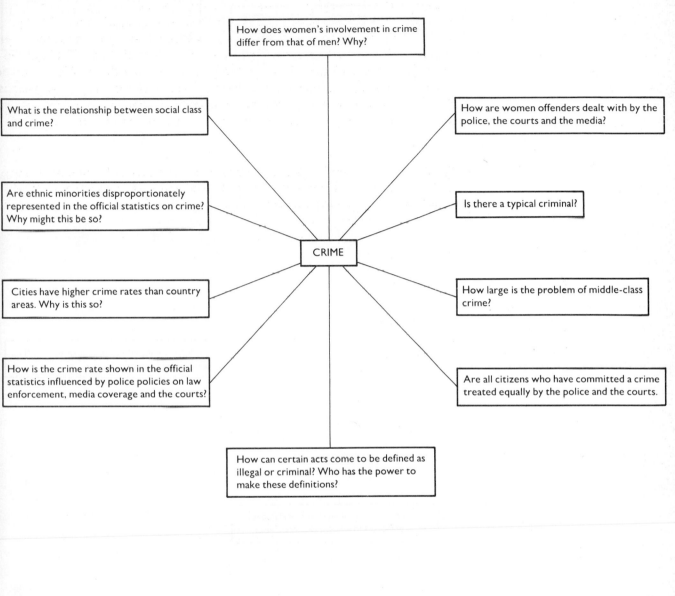

How does women's involvement in crime differ from that of men? Why?

What is the relationship between social class and crime?

How are women offenders dealt with by the police, the courts and the media?

Are ethnic minorities disproportionately represented in the official statistics on crime? Why might this be so?

Is there a typical criminal?

CRIME

Cities have higher crime rates than country areas. Why is this so?

How large is the problem of middle-class crime?

How is the crime rate shown in the official statistics influenced by police policies on law enforcement, media coverage and the courts?

Are all citizens who have committed a crime treated equally by the police and the courts.

How can certain acts come to be defined as illegal or criminal? Who has the power to make these definitions?

What types of football gangs exist? How do they operate?

Is football hooliganism a new problem?

FOOTBALL HOOLIGANISM

How does the media portray football violence? How near is this to reality?

How have the police responded to football hooliganism? How has this affected the 'problem'?

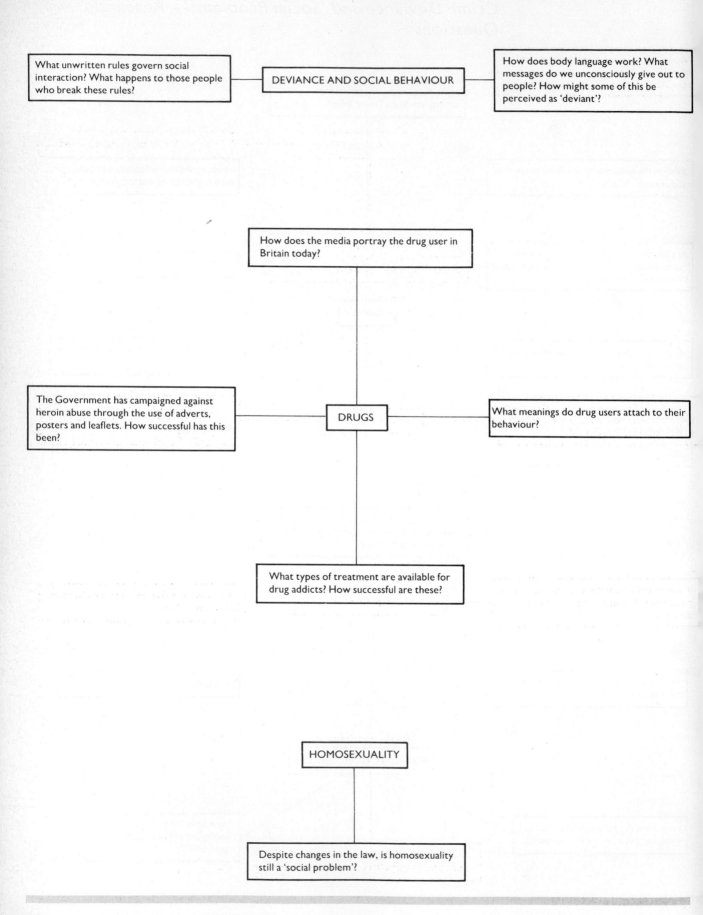

What unwritten rules govern social interaction? What happens to those people who break these rules?

DEVIANCE AND SOCIAL BEHAVIOUR

How does body language work? What messages do we unconsciously give out to people? How might some of this be perceived as 'deviant'?

How does the media portray the drug user in Britain today?

The Government has campaigned against heroin abuse through the use of adverts, posters and leaflets. How successful has this been?

DRUGS

What meanings do drug users attach to their behaviour?

What types of treatment are available for drug addicts? How successful are these?

HOMOSEXUALITY

Despite changes in the law, is homosexuality still a 'social problem'?

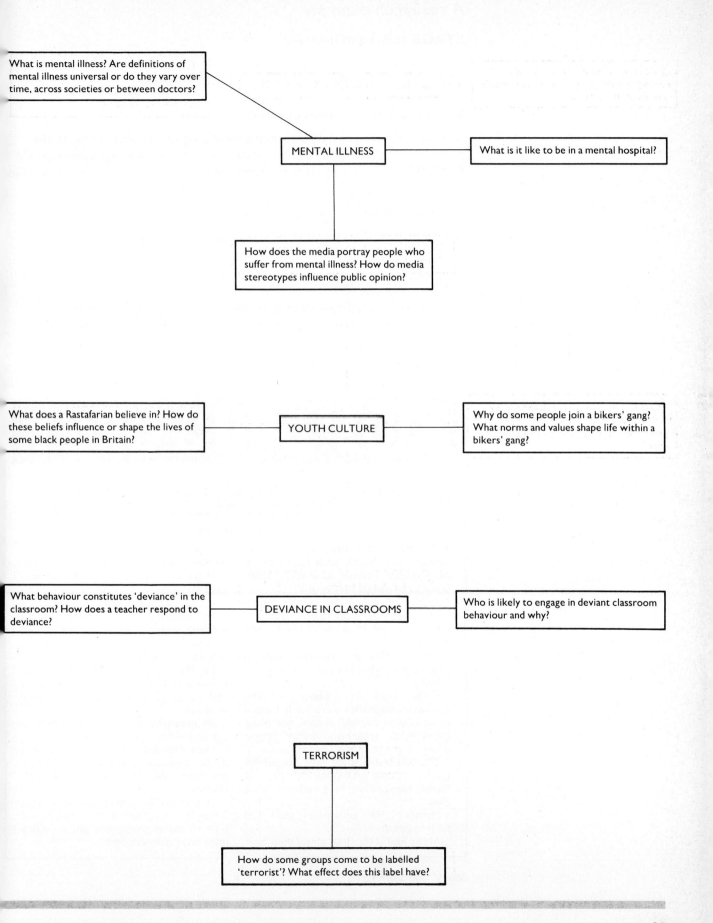

What is mental illness? Are definitions of mental illness universal or do they vary over time, across societies or between doctors?

MENTAL ILLNESS

What is it like to be in a mental hospital?

How does the media portray people who suffer from mental illness? How do media stereotypes influence public opinion?

What does a Rastafarian believe in? How do these beliefs influence or shape the lives of some black people in Britain?

YOUTH CULTURE

Why do some people join a bikers' gang? What norms and values shape life within a bikers' gang?

What behaviour constitutes 'deviance' in the classroom? How does a teacher respond to deviance?

DEVIANCE IN CLASSROOMS

Who is likely to engage in deviant classroom behaviour and why?

TERRORISM

How do some groups come to be labelled 'terrorist'? What effect does this label have?

A research example

STAGE 1: Area of interest

How does the media portray the drug user in Britain?

STAGE 2: Background research

Start by collecting any articles concerning drug takers that appear in the press (national and local) and magazines. Are there any programmes on TV that feature drug taking? Is there anything relevant on national or local radio stations? (*Item A*)

STAGE 3: Writing an hypothesis

From a preliminary look at the sources, the hypothesis is:

The media's portrayal of the drug user is correct.

A definition of exactly what is meant by 'drug user' is needed, for example it could mean someone who abuses illegal drugs or, someone who abuses legal and/or illegal drugs.

Item A

KIDS' DRUG ORGY

Teenies stoned at the toffs' ball

By SUN REPORTER

RICH kids as young as 13 took drugs, got drunk and had sex in disgraceful scenes at a toffs' ball, it was revealed last night.

Girls ran naked through the ballroom while the Acid House drug Ecstasy was sold by a children's charity worker.

Young Hooray Henrys snorted cocaine through rolled-up fivers in toilet cubicles.

Girls aged 13, whose wealthy parents thought they were safely tucked up in bed at friends' homes, got blind drunk while lecherous youths groped them.

The shameful night was staged by tycoon Eddie Davenport, 21, at Shaftesbury's club in London's West End.

Nearly 1,500 youngsters paid £20 each to get in.

Many lied at the door about their age.

Signs throughout the club said drinks would not be served without identity cards proving the holder was over 18.

Booze

But hundreds of youngsters from 13 upwards managed to get sloshed.

Some forked out £20 for a mind-bending tab of Ecstasy.

In the lounge, 14-year-old Laura Crock knocked back a vodka and tonic and said: 'It's no problem getting booze.'

By midnight, youngsters were having sex on the floor in one corner.

Lucy Hendrit, 16-year-old daughter of the drummer of the Kinks, and Ella Sherman, also 16, tore each other's clothes off.

Organiser Davenport, who arrived in a new Bentley, said: 'I can't understand how so many youngsters got in. They must have gate-crashed.'

Source: *The Sun* 4.4.89

DRUGS

»you never know what they'll do to you «

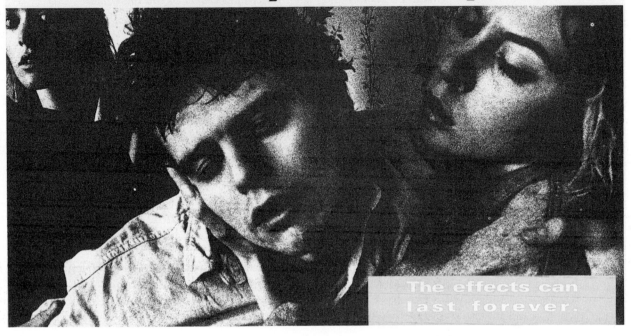

The effects can last forever.

»sometimes the after - effects never wear off«

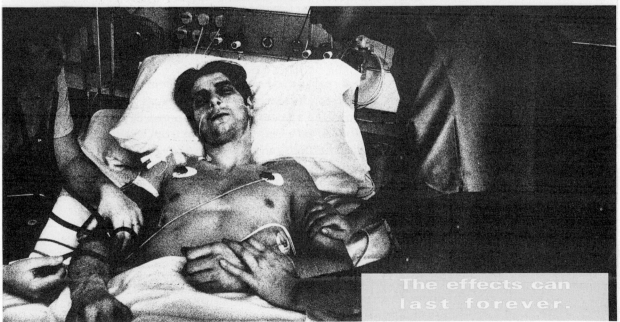

The effects can last forever.

STAGES 4 to 8: Method of enquiry; Detailed planning; Carrying out the research

In using the above hypothesis:

(a) analyse the media's representation of the drug user, and
(b) assess how 'correct' this image is.

Guidance on analysing the media's portrayal of the drug user

According to the newspaper articles, television programmes or advertisements, think about the following:

1. What information/facts are being given about drugs and how they are taken?
2. What types of people use drugs (consider age, gender and social class)?
3. Why do people use drugs?
4. What physical and psychological effects does drug use have on the user?
5. What language is used to desribe the drug user? What effect does it have on the audience?
6. What types of visual images are being used and to what effect?
7. Is drug taking linked with other 'social problems'?
8. In the case of television what sound effects/music are used? What effect does this have on how the audience reacts to certain situations and scenes?
9. What is the impact of drug use on the user's family and friends?
10. What is the overall impression or image of the drug user given by the media? Compile a list of characteristics that make up a 'typical' drug user as presented by the media.

After this investigation assess the extent to which this image is 'correct'. This can be achieved by going to alternative sources of information about drug use.

One possibility is to go to drug users directly. However, think about the following:

- How do you contact them?
- Could you get them to trust you?
- Would you disclose the true purpose of your research?
- Are certain types of drug users more likely to co-operate?

It might be more realistic to contact people from professional agencies who work with drug users, for example social workers, youth workers, counsellors, probation officers. Both questionnaires and/or interviews might be useful methods of gathering information from this sample. Guidance on how to use these methods can be found on pages 81 and 94.

Other alternative sources for information about drug users are:

(i) *Writing to drug information agencies*

ISDD
1-4 Hatton Place
London EC1N 8ND
(Institute for study of drug dependence)

Release
169 Commercial Street
London E1 6BW

Standing Conference on Drug
Abuse
1-4 Hatton Place
London EC1N 8ND

TACADE
1 Hulme Place
The Crescent
Salford
M5 4QA

(ii) *Reading sociological research on drug use*

e.g. Young J., *The drug takers* (MacGibbon and Kee, 1971).
N. Dorne, N. South, *Land fit for heroin* (Macmillan, 1987).
Bailey R.V. and Young J., *Contemporary social problems in Britain* (Saxon House, 1973).

(iii) Diary accounts of drug users

e.g. *Go ask Alice*, Anon. (Corgi, 1973).

(Refer back to 'guidance on analysing data' (p 102) to help you structure your note taking.)

STAGE 9: Analysis of results

From your information you should be able to compare and contrast the image of a drug taker. Set your notes out in a tabular form, to organise your notes, for example:

MEDIA IMAGE	ALTERNATIVE SOURCES
CHARACTERISTICS	
gender	
class	
age	
why they take drugs	
effect on family	

Discuss each point from the table fully, giving examples from both sources.
   Now consider how far you can support your hypothesis. If you cannot, consider *why* the media does not portray an accurate image. Is it deliberate? What effect might this 'false' image have upon the audience?

■ **From your knowledge of methods (refer to Section 1 if necessary) are there any criticisms that you would make of this research example? How could you improve it?**

Presenting your enquiry

Make sure you include:

- A contents page

- An introduction; describe how you moved from your initial area of interest to an hypothesis, including details of any background research, and explain briefly how you intend to carry out your research, giving theoretical and practical reasons for your choice of methods.

- Describe in detail what you did, including your pilot research even if it was later revised completely. It is important to show the process you followed; include your mistakes and discuss what you learned from them.

- Present your results clearly. Include graphs, diagrams, photographs, quotations etc. but only where they add to the text. Include tapes if you have used them but you must still write about them.

- Analyse your results in terms of your hypothesis. Discuss any problems with your research and ideas for further research.

- Include a bibliography and copies of any letters which you have written.

- For some examination boards you have to include a research diary, however, even if this is not required you may still find it useful to do. Record clearly all stages of your research again including any problems and 'mistakes'.

Section 3 · Skills for a Sociology Course

During your course you will be taking notes both in class and from your own reading. It is important to keep a record, because however interesting you may find an article or lesson you are unlikely to remember much of it one or two years later. Also, taking notes involves *thinking* and *selecting* key ideas to record, and to do this you need to *understand* the material. Good note taking is a way of making sense of what you read or hear.

Many students find note taking difficult and because of their uncertainty end up copying out whole articles or chunks from texts, or trying to write down everything the teacher says. This isn't valuable because they have not really 'engaged with' the text or lesson and may not really understand it. Develop a form of note taking which makes you think about what you are writing, which advances your understanding, and which makes sense to you when coming back to it at a later date.

Guidance on note taking

1. In notes from class try to concentrate on *listening* before writing. This way you can select what is important to record.
2. If you are reading a textbook or article you need to skim-read the section first to get a general understanding of what is being said. Then read the section again, but this time underline key pieces of information. After this you are ready to extract these points into your own notes.
3. Avoid taking notes that fill all of the available space on a sheet of A4. Space your work out with a format that is easy to read. Always leave space for any points or questions which you may wish to add later.
4. Underline key words or phrases so that they stand out.
5. Sometimes it is useful to cross reference your notes. This involves making a special note next to a point that links with another topic or argument.
6. You may also want to use arrows or boxes to emphasise a point. Below is an example of a student's notes taken from a newspaper article.

Jill Joliffe reports on the case of the ten-year-old Portuguese girl brought up in a chicken run

Rescue of a wild child

ISABEL QUARESMA is ten, but cannot talk, and is only now learning to eat with a spoon. She is a "wild child" who has only recently been brought into regular contact with human beings.

Isabel's plight was discovered by Conceicao Lobo, a Lisbon journalist who learnt of her story from people in the town of Tabua, close to Portugal's central university city of Coimbra. Since birth the child has lived in a chicken coop. Her mother is a mentally deficient rural worker living in poverty. She has had two other children by members of her own family. Isabel is the only child not born of an incestuous liaison.

The mother works in the fields all day and soon after Isabel's birth confined her to the chicken coop, where she was thrown pieces of bread and shared the chicken-feed with the fowls.

Neighbours had gossiped about this scandal for years, but had done nothing, not wanting to interfere in a family matter.

At last, however, a district hospital worker radiographer at Torres Vedras hospital, approached local institutions to accept Isabel. After a string of refusals, Maria Joao took her into her own home, but could not cope. Isabel's contact with humans had been minimal and she could neither talk nor was she toilet trained — in the chicken coop she had lived in her own excrement.

Her gestures and sounds resembled those of the fowls she had lived with since infancy. She scratched food up with her hands. Defeated, Maria Joao returned the child to her mother.

When Diario de Noticias reported the case, the newspaper faced a similar dilemma — how could a journalist write such a story and then walk away from it? The child was not sick in the strict sense, nor was she mentally deficient, and no institution seemed appropriate — apart from their unwillingness to accept such a difficult case.

Conceicao Lobo finally contacted child psychiatrist Dr Joao dos Santos who removed Isabel from her home.

He had written a paper on Dr Jean Itard's studies of the feral child Victor, found in a French forest in 1800. It was the story on which Francois Truffaut based his film The Wild Child.

Isabel is now at a private clinic for severely handicapped children in Lisbon. It is not ideal because she is still deprived of normal human contact, especially with other children. But she is so severely underdeveloped that she would be unlikely to find the skilled aid she needs outside such an institution.

The most striking thing about her appearance is her severely stunted body. She has a tiny head, and the stature of an infant. X-rays have shown her skull structure to be sound. Her dwarfed form is almost certainly due to a life of malnutrition.

One eye is clouded with a cataract, thought to be the result of a scratch from the hens she lived with. She communicates in repetitive calls and beats her arms and drums her feet to express emotion — actions probably imitative of her only living companions.

Dr Joao dos Santos is optimistic about her chances of social awakening. But he explains : "It all depends on whether we can build warm human contacts which will move her to want to speak and communicate with us."

Source: *The Guardian* 12.6.1980

Rescue of wild child

Guardian 1980, reporter: Jill Joliffe

Story of Isabel – 10 yr old Portuguese girl
— cannot talk, not toilet trained, stunted growth

Background

Her mother is mentally defic., & kept her in a
chicken coop, soon after her birth.
— thrown chicken food & bread ∴ v. poor nutrition
— little contact with other humans ∴ gestures &
sounds just like the chickens she lived with

Main form of communication —
1. repetitive calls 2. beats arms & drums feet

<u>After resale</u>

— now in clinic for severely hardic. children
— not ideal bec. she still doesn't get enough human contact.
— needs skilled staff to help her develop 'human' skills

she presented many officials with a problem bec. she
— was not really 'sick'
— not mentally defic. either

↓ ↓

* her condition was the result of not *
being socialised like other children.
she had not learned to talk & play
* like other children. *

(left margin, rotated): evidence of the import. of socialisation process i.e. we learn to be human. — see notes on socialisation theory. *

PROJECTS

1. Using the section on social surveys, take notes in the form of a flow chart to illustrate the different stages in planning and carrying out a social survey. For each point show why it is important and illustrate where possible with examples. **Try to do this on one side of A4 paper.**

2. Read and take notes from 'Peter Townsend and the Holy Grail' by David Piachaud in *New Society* 10 September 1981. Use these notes to discuss whether Townsend's research on poverty (pages 19-24) has provided an 'objective measure of relative poverty'.

3. Using at least three of the studies in Section One of this book make notes in preparation for answering the following essay question:
    'Values must inevitably enter research in many ways, from the choice of topic to be studied, through the formulation of hypotheses and methodology adopted, to the final interpretation of the data. Discuss.'
    Be careful to structure your notes in relation to the title.

4. Take brief notes from the following article to show how you could use it to illustrate the claim that official statistics are social constructs.

'Fewer out of work'

OUT OF 24 changes in the unemployment figures since October 1979, counted by the Unemployment Unit (UU), a research and pressure group, only one has raised the official measure of unemployment — the first. Since then, it has been down, down, down.

The Department itself concedes that the definition of unemployment in the monthly official count has changed a number of times, but says that each one must be looked at on its merits. There is no deliberate policy of reducing the count.

It also argues, quite rightly, that there is no unique definition of unemployment. The monthly count merely takes people who claim benefits and are in theory looking for work. But each year there is also an EC-sponsored Labour Force Survey, based on a very large sample, which provides an independent assessment of unemployment defined as anyone who looked for work in the last four weeks — the International Labour Office definition.

The latest LFS figures published on Sunday show that most of the recent drop in unemployment has been genuine. The fall in the number of jobless between the LFS in the spring of 1987 and the spring of 1988 (the latest figure) was 505,000 compared with a drop of 540,000 on the official count.

The level of unemployment on the LFS definition is put at 2.37 million last spring, compared with 2.41 million on the claimant count. Employment Secretary Norman Fowler immediately claimed that the results "confirm the position recorded in the monthly benefit". However, the truth is that the two definitions are measuring such widely different things that any similarity is purely coincidental.

For example, some 750,000 people found by the LFS to be unemployed were not claiming benefit at all. And some 790,000 claiming benefit were not unemployed — 160,000 were employed and another 630,000 had not looked for work.

Nevertheless, the LFS figures are not what receives public attention. They provide a useful benchmark but they are only published once a year and then only after a considerable delay. For most purposes, the official monthly count is what matters. And that definition has been changed radically.

It is getting more and more difficult to establish what the "old" monthly definition before 1982 would have shown. But for what it is worth the Unemployment Unit publishes an est-imate each month. Instead of an official total which just sneaked below 2 million in January — 1,988,100 — the UU believes that the old figure would have been 2,678,900.

In both cases, the figure would be reduced by special employment measures such as the Community programme, or by people going on to training schemes such as the YTS. Some people like to add those figures on too, to get even higher totals.

The UU lists the following changes which have affected the official unemployment count since 1979:

● **October 1979.** Change to fortnightly payment of benefits. Effect: plus 20,000.

● **October 1979.** Compensating adjustment to published seasonally-adjusted totals. Effect: minus 20,000.

● **February 1981.** First published estimate of register effect of special employment and training measures. The coverage had been increased from 250,000 participants at the start of 1979 to 668,000 by January 1986. Effect: minus 370,000 and minus 495,000 by January 1986.

● **July-October 1981.** Seasonally adjusted figures for these months reduced by 20,000 to compensate for effect on count of emergency procedures to deal with DHSS strikes. Effect: minus 20,000.

● **July 1981.** Unemployed men aged 60 and above drawing benefit for over a year given option of higher long-term rate in return for not registering for work. Effect: minus 30,000 by May 1982.

● **July 1982.** Taxation of unemployment benefit. This may have cut the count by encouraging single parents to switch to untaxed supplementary benefit.

● **October 1982.** Change in definition and compilation of monthly unemployment figures from a clerical count of people registered for work at Job-Centres and careers offices to a computer count covering only benefit claimants. Effect: minus 170,000 to 190,000 adults and minus 26,000 school-leavers.

● **April 1983.** Men aged 60 and over and not entitled to benefit no longer required to sign on at benefit offices to get NI credits. Effect: minus 107,400 by June 1983.

● **June 1983.** All men aged 60 and over allowed long-term supplementary benefit as soon as they come on to supplementary benefit. Effect: minus 54,400 by August 1983.

● **June 1983.** Because school leavers cannot claim benefit until September, between 100,000 and 200,000 are missed from the June, July and August figures.

● **October 1984.** Community programme restricted solely to unemployed benefit claimants. Effect: minus 29,000 by January 1986.

● **July 1985.** Reconciliation of Northern Ireland records with computer records. Effect: minus 5,000.

● **July 1985.** Payment of unemployment benefit in arrears. No estimate.

● **March 1986.** Introduction of a two-week delay in publishing the monthly count to "improve accuracy". Effect: minus 40,000 to 90,000, average minus 50,000.

● **June 1986.** New method of calculating unemployment rate using larger denominator which includes unemployed. Effect: minus 1 to 1.5 percentage points.

● **June 1986** onwards. Restart interviews combined with tighter available-for-work test. Both further tightened in 1988. Effect: minus 200,000 to 300,000 in 1988.

● **October 1986.** Abolition of right to partial unemployment benefit for people with low NI contributions. Effect: minus 24,000 after one year; minus 30,000 after two.

● **October 1986.** Voluntary unemployment deduction to unemployment benefit extended from 6 weeks to 13 weeks. Effect: minus 2,000 to 3,000.

● **April 1988.** Voluntary unemployment deduction to Unemployment Benefit extended from 13 weeks to 26 weeks. Effect: minus 12,000.

● **April 1988.** Small reduction due to ability of unemployed to claim income support while undertaking part-time work.

● **June 1988.** New larger denominator used in calculating unemployment rate. Effect: minus 0.1 percentage point.

● **September 1988.** Section 4 of 1988 Social Security Act denies benefit to all 16 and 17-year-olds which remove them from the count. Effect: minus 90,000 to 120,000.

● **October 1988.** Section 6 of Act amends contribution conditions for short-term benefits. Effect: minus 38,000.

● **October 1988.** Section 7 of Act lowers age limit for abatement of unemployment benefit to occupational pensioners from 60 to 55. Effect: minus 30,000.

● **September 1989?** Clauses 7 and 10 of 1988 Social Security Bill make it a condition that to receive benefit as unemployed, claimants must be able to prove they are actively seeking work. Clause 9 of Bill proposes that after a period the level of pay will not be good cause for turning down a job. Effect: minus 50,000?   C.H.

Source: *The Guardian* 15.3.1989

Writing sociology essays

Essay questions are designed to test not just what you know but also your understanding of an issue and your ability to apply your knowledge and understanding to a specific question. Selective use of evidence to support your arguments is very important.

When writing essays it is vital to answer the question that is being asked rather than writing everything you know about a topic, or answering the question you would like to be set. There are certain basic stages in preparing and writing a good essay;

- Work out exactly what the question is asking you to do. Underline key words. Make sure that you understand all of the terms being used, e.g. 'white collar crime', 'economic deprivation', 'gender-role socialisation.'

- Identify the different sides to the argument you are being asked to discuss.

- Read and take notes from textbooks, class notes, relevant articles, etc.

- Go back to the question and organise your notes to develop an argument.

- Plan your paragraphs. Identify the separate points and the order in which you want to discuss them. Decide on the evidence and examples you will use to illustrate your points.

- Write an introduction for your essay. Keep this fairly brief. You must identify the key issues raised by the question and define any concepts used in the title, but don't answer the whole question. A good introduction will provide a structure for the rest of your essay. (See the example on page 110.)

- Write your essay in rough. Refer back to the question during your essay, and make sure that you link your paragraphs together so that your argument flows. Use key phrases to link paragraphs, e.g., 'Another argument could be', 'Conflicting evidence is provided by', 'These arguments have been developed and modified by'.

   Support your arguments with evidence from different sources and use sociological evidence, *not* your personal experiences or prejudices. Make sure that the evidence you use actually adds to the argument; avoid illustrating the same point several times.

   If you quote from texts always do so briefly and always acknowledge the source. Never copy out chunks from books.

   Try to write clearly and simply, and only use technical terms if you fully understand them.

   In your conclusion refer back to the question and sum up your discussion. Avoid over-simplifying the debate and don't be afraid to raise more issues or questions. (See the example on page 111.)

- Read through your essay critically. Cross out any points which are irrelevant or repetitive. Does the essay as a whole answer the question set?

   When you are satisfied with your essay rewrite it.

- Include a list of sources used in planning your essay (a bibliography).

Writing essays in timed conditions

The technique for writing timed essays and examination essays should be very similar to classwork/homework essays. Obviously you will not do any reading, use your notes or write your essay in rough first, but careful planning is essential and it is well worth spending a few minutes on this. It is very important in your essays to explain all of your points and not assume that the examiner will know what you mean.

An example of a well-planned essay

'Racism is the major explanation for the disadvantages experienced by ethnic minorities in industrial societies'

Introduction

Racism can be defined as the belief that certain races are superior to others, and as such some groups are therefore justified in having power and privilege above other groups. The quote in the title suggests that racism is the major explanation for disadvantages. To find out if this is true we need firstly to look at alternative explanations for them.

Sections to essay

Work ⟶ Describe disadvantages
Housing ⟶ Evidence - E.G. PEP Report
Explanations — Functionalist
— Marxist
— Weber

Historical change
Race Discrim. Act

Education — Describe disadvantages
— Evidence E.G. Swann Report
— Explanations — Interactionist
— Marxist
Recent Changes — Multi cultural
Anti-Racist strategies

Eq. of Opport?

Police + Law enforcement
— Evidence — Scarman Report/Riots
1981/83
— Recommendations

CONCLUSION — While there can be no doubt about the nature of disadvantage that is experienced by ethnic minority groups, discussion still rages about the cause of these disadvantages. More conservative commentators would argue that equality of opportunity is with us. It just takes time. Other perhaps more left wing writers would argue that racism is still a very powerful force restraining the advancement of ethnic minorities in Britain. Indeed, some would go so far as to say that their exploitation is crucial for the survival of capitalism.

■ **PROJECTS**

Use the essay titles on methodology on page 65 to answer these questions.

1. **Select two essays to write an introduction for; be careful to define the concepts used and set up the main themes of the essays. Write a detailed plan and conclusion for these essays. Show your work to someone on your course. Do they agree that you have interpreted the question correctly? Could they improve your plan?**

2. **Select one essay. Use the relevant sections in this book, your class notes and at least one textbook to prepare for it. If you can, discuss your plan with other sociology students before writing the essay.**

3. **Select an essay title and prepare a detailed plan to present to the rest of your class. Be prepared to explain your plan fully and to answer any questions.**

4. **Select a different essay and write a 'note form answer' in twenty minutes.**

5. **Revise all of your notes on methodology, ask someone to choose an essay for you to write in forty-five minutes. Read through your answer. Where could it be improved?**

Common words used in essay and stimulus questions

describe, outline This requires you to explain a set of ideas or arguments. Very few questions will ask you just to describe.

evaluate, critically evaluate, assess, critically assess, outline and assess Discuss the strengths and weaknesses of an approach or argument. This involves first *outlining* the theory or viewpoint you are asked to discuss, then looking at the theoretical and empirical evidence both supporting and criticising the theory. It is important that you reach a conclusion.

discuss This usually follows a quotation – look at both sides of the argument using empirical evidence. It is quite common for students to take a quotation and present just the argument and evidence for it. To discuss an issue you need to look at the other side even if you reject it.

compare and contrast What do the approaches have in common (compare) and in what ways do they differ (contrast)? It is quite easy just to focus on one side especially when, for example, the theories don't, on the surface, seem to have much in common.

explain, account for, examine State in detail a particular approach or argument, identifying its significance.

illustrate with examples Back up your arguments with relevant empirical examples.

to what extent, how useful How far does an approach or argument help us to understand an issue? Weigh up the positive contributions and gaps in the approach. Draw upon alternative approaches to complete an understanding of an issue.

what are the implications This often follows a statement or quotation. What does this mean or how does it affect the situation under discussion?

what are the limitations What are the problems with this view? Where are the weaknesses?

All your arguments should be backed up with examples, even when it isn't directly asked for.

Answering stimulus questions

Most Examination Boards now set stimulus response questions alongside traditional essay-type questions. The aim of these questions is to test your ability to use and evaluate evidence rather than merely to reproduce knowledge. The type of stimulus provided is wide-ranging, including extracts from sociology texts, articles from newspapers or magazines, cartoons, and statistical information in the form of tables, graphs or pie charts. Often several different extracts will be provided for comparison and evaluation. The questions which you have to answer can vary. In some cases the majority of the marks may be gained by using the evidence provided, but more often they also include questions related to the stimulus but requiring knowledge which is not in the extracts, rather like mini essay questions. It is important that you look at, and practise, examples of questions which are set by the Examination Board whose examination you will be taking.

For all types of stimulus questions there are certain basic points to consider when preparing and writing your answer:

- Read the passage and all of the questions carefully twice. On second reading, underline the key points in the passage in relation to the questions.

- If the questions are divided up into different parts, answer them as separate questions, showing clearly in the margin which part of the question you are answering. For each section make sure that you include only information that is relevant to that part of the question – accurate responses to part (b) in your answer to (d) will not gain marks.

- Pay attention to the way marks are divided up between sections. If a question is only worth two or three marks you do not need to write long detailed answers. Often answers to small questions will take the form of a brief list of points. If a question is worth ten marks out of a total of twenty-five you should spend about a third of your time on it and write one and a half to two sides.

- *Use* the material which is given to you in the extracts. The marks for the smaller questions can often be gained from a very careful reading of this material.

- Plan your answers carefully. Your plans for stimulus questions are not likely to be as long as for essays, but it is still important to identify the key themes and to plan your argument carefully for the mini essay questions.

- Pay particular attention to the way the questions are worded (see the list of common words used on page 112) and make sure that you do what the question asks for.

- Answer the questions set, not the questions you would have liked to have been asked.

Stimulus Questions: Example I

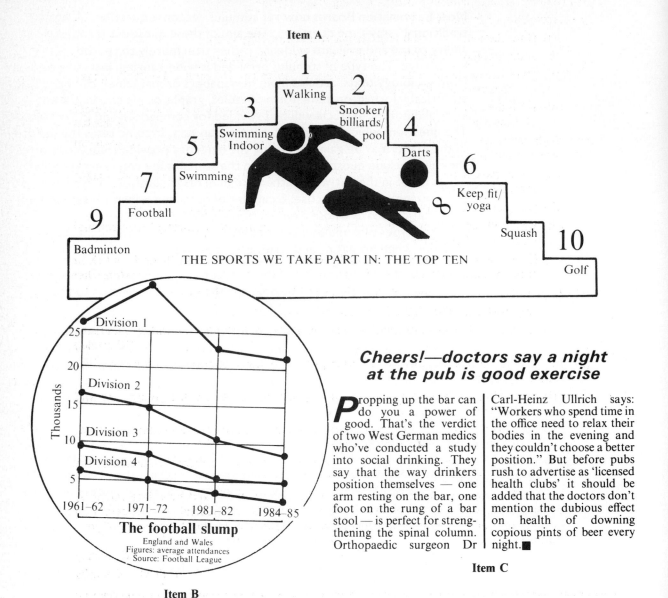

Item A

1 Walking
2 Snooker/billiards/pool
3 Swimming Indoor
4 Darts
5 Swimming
6 Keep fit/yoga
7 Football
8 Squash
9 Badminton
10 Golf

THE SPORTS WE TAKE PART IN: THE TOP TEN

Item B

Division 1
Division 2
Division 3
Division 4

Thousands

1961–62   1971–72   1981–82   1984–85

The football slump

England and Wales
Figures: average attendances
Source: Football League

Cheers!—doctors say a night at the pub is good exercise

Propping up the bar can do you a power of good. That's the verdict of two West German medics who've conducted a study into social drinking. They say that the way drinkers position themselves — one arm resting on the bar, one foot on the rung of a bar stool — is perfect for strengthening the spinal column. Orthopaedic surgeon Dr Carl-Heinz Ullrich says: "Workers who spend time in the office need to relax their bodies in the evening and they couldn't choose a better position." But before pubs rush to advertise as 'licensed health clubs' it should be added that the doctors don't mention the dubious effect on health of downing copious pints of beer every night.■

Item C

	Percentage engaging in each activity in the 4 weeks before interview		
	Professional employers and managers	Semi- and unskilled manual	Full time students
Golf	7	0	3
Swimming indoor	9	4	17
Squash	6	1	8
Darts	6	7	12
Billiards/snooker	9	6	18
Walking (2 miles or more)	24	14	18

(Source: Social Trends, 1986)

Item D

SECTION A

1. Study Items A to D carefully before starting this question.

    (*a*) According to Items A to D:

    (i) state the activity which is participated in most frequently;

    (ii) state the activity which is participated in least frequently;

    (iii) state the decrease in average attendance figures for Division 1 Football League matches between 1961 and 1985;

    (iv) state the activity which seems to be most equally engaged in by both professional and manual groups.   **(4 marks)**

    (*b*) With reference to Items A to D give a brief critical assessment of any sociological research method which might be used to investigate:

    (i) the apparent decline, as in Item B, in the popularity of going to watch league football matches;

    (ii) whether social drinking, as in Item C, may be viewed as good exercise;

    (iii) why golf, as in Item D, does not seem to be an activity associated with manual workers and students;

    (iv) if television coverage has increased peoples' participation, as in Items A and D, in snooker and/or darts.   **(16 marks)**

    (*c*) Explain fully which Item might be considered by a sociologist as:

    (i) the most objective, factual and accurate information;

    (ii) the most subjective information which probably reflects opinion rather than facts.

                                                                                   (10 marks)

    (*d*) Imagine that it has been decided to attempt a sociological enquiry into any *one* of the following topics:

    (i) the difference in leisure pursuits, including sports, between the young men and women in your educational institution;

    (ii) the effects of large companies promoting sporting activities and major national events through sponsorship schemes;

    (iii) the investigation of the availability of, and demand for, leisure provisions for the area in which you now live.

    Show briefly what your starting points are for such a study, and how data might be collected, organised and presented in a coherent and purposeful way. Attempt to identify and make use of sociological concepts. Be careful to specify the scale of your study. Factors such as costs and time allowance should be considered.

                                                                                   (20 marks)
                                                                         TOTAL: 50 marks

(London A/S Level Specimen paper 1988)

Example I Guidelines

You have approximately one hour and ten minutes for this question. Before you start spend at least ten minutes reading the extracts and questions and underlining key points. The guidance given on the marks available for each part enables you to work out how to divide up your time.

Q.1a   All four marks can be gained by reading the tables carefully. One word answers are perfectly acceptable; there is no need to write full sentences for questions like this.

Q.1b   You have about twenty minutes to answer all four parts of this question so it is crucial to write only relevant points. For each part
   – identify a suitable research method
   – explain why it is suited to this topic
   – what are its problems for this topic?
It is quite possible to use the same method more than once but your points will be different because you must relate it to a particular topic of research. You don't just have to use primary methods of research, you may use a variety of types of secondary data.

Q.1c   It is not enough just to state the right answer, you must say *why*. You need to look closely at each extract to see how the information was collected
   – is the source reliable?
   – how might bias or error have entered?
Data based on a sample is less accurate than data which includes all relevant people. Data based on interviews could introduce error because people may not tell the truth either because they have forgotten or because they do not wish to admit that they do no exercise.

Q.1d   Choose a question which you could investigate easily. Time is fairly limited but you should spend a couple of minutes writing a quick plan before you start.
   Plan for 1d (i)
      Hypothesis
      Method – Questionnaire – Why? (Time, money, access)
      Size of sample (Time cost)
      How to get a random sample (Stratified sample equal m/f)
      Type of Q's (mostly closed)
      Pilot survey – Why?
      Analysis (relate back to hyp., compare m/f)
      Poss. project diary.

■ **ACTIVITY**
Bearing these points in mind, write an answer to this question in one hour and ten minutes.

Stimulus Questions: Example 2

Item A

The middle-class parents take more interest in their children's progress at school than the manual working-class parents do, and they become relatively more interested as their children grow older. They visit the school more frequently to find out how their children are getting on with their work, and when they do are more likely to ask to see the Head as well as the class teacher, whereas the manual working-class parents are usually content to see the class teacher only. In this study, the level of the parents' interest in their children's work was partly based on comments made by the class teachers and partly on the records on the number of times each parent visited the schools to discuss their child's progress with the Head or class teacher. At both eight and 11 years, but particularly at 11, the highest average scores in the tests are made by the children whose parents are the most interested in their education and the lowest by those whose parents are the least interested.

(*The Home and the School*, J. W. B. Douglas)

Item B

The following extract is from tape recordings made by a young teacher in her first term of teaching in an inner-city New York elementary school with a high Negro/Puerto Rican enrolment.

Mrs Jones, the 6th-grade teacher, and I were discussing reading problems. I said, 'I wonder about my children. They don't seem too slow; they seem average. Some of them even seem to be above average. I can't understand how they can grow up to be 5th and 6th graders and still be reading on the 2nd grade level. It seems absolutely amazing.' Mrs Jones (an experienced teacher) explained about environmental problems that these children have. 'Some of them never see a newspaper. Some of them have never been on a subway. The parents are so busy having parties and things that they have no time for their children. They can't even take them to a museum or anything.' . . . You have to remember that in a school such as ours the children are not as ready and willing to learn as in schools in middle-class neighbourhoods.

(How Teachers Learn to Help Children Fail',
E. Fuchs in *Tinker, Tailor*, ed. N. Keddie)

Item C

Stanworth's (1983) analysis of 'A' level classes reports that, from the pupils' point of view, it is boys who stand out vividly in classroom interaction. Boys are, according to the pupils' reports, four times more likely than girls to join in discussion, or to offer comments in class. They are twice as likely to demand help or attention from the teacher, and twice as likely to be seen as 'model pupils'.

These sorts of differences were of equal relevance in the classes taught by women teachers. Boys were still the focus of attention. In addition, teachers reported that they identified more readily with boys and were more attached to them. They were more likely to reject girls and often assumed routinely that they would not pursue their studies because of marriage.

(Adapted from *Education*, Stephen Ball)

(a) What criticisms could be made of the method, described in *Item A*, which is used to measure parents' interest in their children's work? (4 marks)

(b) Illustrating your answer with material from *Items A* and *B*, explain what is meant by 'cultural deprivation'. (6 marks)

(c) How useful is the concept of cultural deprivation to an understanding of differences in educational achievement? (7 marks)

(d) Using material from *Item C* and elsewhere, examine the influence of the hidden curriculum on gender differences in education. (8 marks)

(AEB A Level Specimen paper 1989)

Example 2 Guidelines

Section A

- Underline key words in the passage and the corresponding relevant information in the extract.
- Identify what method was used. Was this the most accurate way to measure interest? What are the problems with this method?

- Note there are only four marks for this section, so don't get carried away. Keep it brief.

Section B

- Define 'cultural deprivation'.
- Give examples from *Item A* and *Item B*.

Section C

- Evaluate the concept of cultural deprivation. State *how* it has been used to explain underachievement. Locate it within a sociological perspective.
- Be careful not to repeat information given in Section B.
- What are the problems with this concept?
- Give an alternative explanation for underachievement.

Section D

How important is the hidden curriculum in influencing gender differences in schools?

- Define 'hidden curriculum' and 'gender'.
- Remember to discuss males and females.
- State what gender differences exist.
- Give examples from *Item C*.
- Add new material that supports the notion that the hidden curriculum is important.
- What other things could influence gender differences?

Example 3

Item A

Offenders found guilty of, or cautioned for, indictable offences: by sex, and type of offence, 1984, England and Wales

	All ages males (thousands)	All ages females (thousands)
Indictable offences (percentages)		
Murder, manslaughter, or infanticide	0.3	0.1
Other violence against the person	50.1	5.2
Sexual offences	8.2	0.1
Burglary	83.2	3.1
Robbery	4.3	0.2
Theft and handling stolen goods	240.0	71.5
Fraud and forgery	21.4	6.2
Criminal damage	13.0	1.0
Other indictable (excluding motoring) offences	30.5	3.9
Indictable motoring offences	28.1	1.0
Total indictable offences	479.0	92.3
Number of offenders per 1,000 population	23	4

Source: adapted from Social Trends 1986. (HMSO)

Item B

As part of her research into female delinquency, Lesley Shacklady Smith asked three samples of teenage girls to complete a self-report questionnaire. The control group were girls who had never been referred to a juvenile court, the probation sample were girls who had received probation or supervision orders and the gang sample were girls belonging to delinquent gangs. In each case 'N' is the number of girls who completed the questionnaires.

Reported delinquent behaviour among girls in three samples

Type of offence	Control sample N = 30 %	Probation sample N = 30 %	Gang sample N = 15 %
Skipped school	63.3	90.0	93.3
Taken articles from a shop	36.7	90.0	80.0
Breaking and entering	10.0	33.3	26.7
Been in a car without the owner's permission	16.7	60.0	60.0
Deliberate property damage	26.7	66.7	73.3
Runaway from home	3.3	70.0	53.3
Had sex relations under age of age of consent with person of opposite sex	13.3	70.0	73.3
Taken drugs	3.3	10.0	33.3
Taken part in fight	23.3	63.3	73.3

Source: *Sexist assumptions and female delinquency*, Lesley Shacklady Smith.

Item C

In her study *The Girls in the Gang* (1984, Blackwell) Anne Campbell used informal interviews to investigate the roles girls play in American gangs. The sections in italic are the questions Anne Campbell asked.

I'm glad I got a reputation. That way nobody will start with me, you know. They're going to come out losing. Like all of us, we got a reputation. We're crazy, nobody wants to fight us for that reason – you know. They say, 'No man. That girl might stab me or cut my face or something like that.' (The Turban Queens)

And you had guns then as well. You were taking night work, you were doing robberies, something like that?
Uh-huh, but, you know, I used to make myself look like a boy. It was easy for a girl to do that, and then I could change back and be, you know, a little feminine girl again. So that's another way I used to get over too.
Yeah, 'cos if anybody saw you they'd say, 'Oh there's this young boy.'
Never think it was me. Well, I remember, every time we'd do something slick, I used to have to look like a boy.
Useful sometimes.
Put your braids up in your hat, specially wintertime. Boy, Mimi would say, 'Better put them braids up, better put them up.'
And you thought that if you kept hanging around doing what you were doing, you might have gotten shot one day?
Yeah, I mean I had guns and stuff, you know? Here, alright, in New York City, up here in Manhattan, Brooklyn, Queens, and all that, guns originate from a lot of gang wars and stuff like that. (Sun Africa from the Puma Crew)

Then everybody started doubling up on one girl. We hurt them up 'cos the girl had to go to hospital 'cos her teeth were messed up. Noreen had her on the floor. Noreen was over her and I said, 'Noreen, I'm going to kick her.' Noreen was saying, 'Don't kick her in the mouth,' you know? I just started kicking her mouth, I wasn't really caring, and she got hurt up by her gums. I guess they were sore and we did see blood. These girls told us that they had to go to the hospital. We had bottles, knives, and everything, 'cos nobody had a gun. We won and it was so bad. (Sun Africa from the Puma Crew)

1. According to *Item A*
   (a) In 1984 what was the total number of males convicted
       for indictable offences?   (2 marks)
   (b) In 1984 what was the total number of females convicted
       for indictable offences?   (2 marks)
2. How does the picture of female crime shown in *Item B* differ
   from that shown in *Item A*?   (4 marks)
3. Some groups of people are more likely to be convicted for
   their crime than others. What explanations have sociologists
   offered to account for this?   (6 marks)
4. Critically evaluate the type of evidence provided in each of
   the three extracts.   (13 marks)

Preparing for your examinations

Organising your notes

Ideally you should organise your notes for revision when you finish a topic and not leave it until just before the exam.

- Read through all of your notes on a topic and make sure that they are complete. Now is the time to do any reading that you neglected to do earlier on. If you don't really understand any of your notes go and ask your teacher or other students to explain them.
- As you read through your notes try to identify *key issues* and any supporting *empirical evidence*. Looking at past exam papers might help. Try to write these key issues out on one sheet of paper either as a flow diagram or as a list, showing how the different issues are linked.
- Make a list on a separate sheet of paper of all the concepts or specialist terms such as, 'hidden curriculum', 'proletariat' or 'underclass'. Write out brief definitions of these terms.
- Rewrite your notes in abbreviated form to fit the key issues you have identified. This might involve reorganising your notes quite considerably.
- Make any cross references in your notes to other topics which you have studied.

Learning from your revision notes

- Plan your revision time carefully, a definite timetable would help. Don't leave everything to the last minute.
- Start off with a topic that you feel comfortable with to help you master the revision technique.
- Find somewhere quiet and comfortable.
- Work for short periods initially. Be honest with yourself, if you have lost your concentration, take a break.
- Test your knowledge and understanding frequently by writing essay plans, introductions to essays and timed answers to different types of questions. Don't just choose the questions you can do easily. It is important to test not just whether you have learned your notes but also whether you understand and can apply them.
- Often it helps to work with other people, discussing approaches to questions etc.

Examination technique

- Read the whole paper carefully before you start. Only select questions which you fully understand.
- When you have chosen a question, underline any key words and plan your answer carefully (see p 109 for essay plans and p 113 for plans for stimulus questions). Your plan should identify the key arguments but should not argue them, plans which are as long as the essay waste time. Remember to refer back to your plan frequently when you write your essay.
- Leave a space at the end of each answer to allow for anything you want to add later if you have any time left.
- Organise your time carefully to answer the right number of questions.
- If you do run out of time, write an extended plan for your last essay, but to gain marks you must not just give a list of names or concepts; you must explain briefly how you would use them.
- If you have any time left at the end of the exam, re-read your answers and improve them if possible.

Addresses for Examination Boards

Joint Matriculation Board
Manchester
M15 6EU

Associated Examining Board
Stag Hill House
Guildford
Surrey
GU2 5XJ

University of London Schools Examinations Board
Stewart House
32 Russell Square
London
WC1B 5DN

University of Cambridge Local Examinations Syndicate
Syndicate Buildings
1 Hills Road
Cambridge
CB1 2EU

University of Oxford Delagacy of Local Examinations
Ewert Place
Summertown
Oxford
OX2 7BZ

All of these Examination Boards offer A-level sociology. In addition AEB and London also offer A/S-level.

Resources for the sociologist

Textbooks

There are a number of good sociology textbooks available. You should use one basic textbook, although you may want to 'dip into' another one for some topics. Use the contents pages of different textbooks to find out which areas of the syllabus they cover.

Topic books

These are increasingly common, covering just one area of the syllabus such as crime, religion or the family. Many are very good and well worth looking at.

Readers

These are collections of articles, or extracts from original sociological works. The extracts have usually been carefully selected to cover a range of issues and are usually suitable for A- and A/S-level students. They provide a good overview of primary research.

Original texts

If you have time it is always worth reading sociology books themselves rather than textbook accounts of them. This is particularly true of books based on sociological research which are often very readable and give an insight into how sociology is done.

Journals

Journals are excellent for providing up-to-date information on a topic or for details of research which is being done now. The *Social Studies Review* (published three times a year by Phillip Allan Publishers) is particularly useful. This is written for A-level students of Sociology and Political studies and includes a good range of articles and also examples of A-level essays with examiners' comments. *New Society*, which is published weekly, is also useful and there is an index which will allow you to find relevant articles.

Statistics

Statistics are available from a number of sources, *Social Trends* (published annually by HMSO) is a particularly useful collection of statistics on all aspects of social life. You do need to be aware of problems associated with using statistics (see pages 43-47).

Newspapers

Newspapers can be a useful source of topical information but you should always remember the question of bias in the media (see page 47).

General Bibliography

Anon., *Go ask Alice*, Corgi, 1973

Bailey R.V. and Young J., *Contemporary Social Problems in Britain*, Saxon House, 1973

Ball S., *Education*, Longman, 1986

Barker E., *The Making of a Moonie – Choice or Brainwashing*, Basil Blackwell, 1984

Campbell A., *The Girls in the Gang*, Basil Blackwell, 1984

Centre for Football Research, *Young People's Images of Attending Football: A Preliminary Analysis*, Leicester University, 1987

Dobash R.E. and Dobash R. *Violence against wives*, Open Books Ltd 1979

Dorn N. and South N., *Land Fit for Heroin: Drug Policies, Prevention and Practice*, Macmillan Education, 1987

Douglas J.W.B., *The Home and the School*, Panther, 1964

The Elton Report on School Discipline, Sheffield University Educational Research Centre, 1989

Glasgow Media Group, *War and Peace News*, Open University Press, 1985

Grabrucker M., *There's a Good Girl*, Women's Press Ltd, 1989

Humphreys L., *Tearoom Trade*, Duckworth and Company Ltd, 1970

Keddie N. (Ed), *Tinker Tailor: the Myth of Cultural Deprivation*, Penguin, 1969

Oakley A., *From Here to Maternity*, Penguin, 1981

One Day I'll Have My Own Place To Stay: Young Homeless People Write About Their Lives, Central London Social Security Advisers Forum 1989

Patrick J., *A Glasgow Gang Observed*, Eyre Methuen Ltd, 1973

Townsend P. and Davidson, *Inequalities in Health*, Penguin, 1982

Townsend P., *Poverty in the United Kingdom: A survey of Household Resources and Standards of Living*, Penguin, 1979

Whitehead M., *The Health Divide*, Penguin, 1988

Willmott P., *Friendship Networks and Social Support*, Policy Studies Institute, 1987

Young J., *The Drugtakers: the Social Meaning of Drug Use*, MacGibbon and Kee, 1971.

Index

Acknowledgements

The authors and publishers would like to thank the following:

for permission to reproduce text extracts:

The Associated Examining Board for examination questions, pp 65, 118.

Basil Blackwell for extracts from *The Making of A Moonie*, by Eileen Barker, 1984, pp 60-62 and extracts from *The Girls in the Gang* by Anne Campbell, 1984, p 120.

Madelaine Bunting for 'Waterloo homeless beg for change at the end of the line', p 91.

Stephen Cook for 'Growing army of beggars in London', p 91.

Curtis Brown Group Ltd for extracts from *From Here to Maternity*, © Ann Oakley 1981, pp 30-34.

Duckworth and Company Limited for extracts from *Tearoom Trade* by L. Humphreys 1970, pp 12-13.

The Football Trust-funded Centre for Football Research for extracts from *Young People's Images of Attending Football: A Preliminary Analysis of Essays by Liverpool School Children*, 1987, pp 53-56.

The Guardian for 'Fewer out of work', p 108.

The Controller of Her Majesty's Stationery Office for extracts from *Inequalities in Health* by Townsend and Davidson, 1982, pp 44-46 and *The Elton Report on School Discipline*, 1989, p 73.

The Joint Matriculation Board for examination questions, p 65.

Jill Joliffe for 'Rescue of a wild child', p 106.

Methuen London for extracts from *A Glasgow Gang Observed* by James Patrick, pp 10-11.

Open Books Publishing Limited for extracts from *Violence Against Wives* by Dobash and Dobash, pp 35-41.

Open University Press for extracts from *War and Peace News* by the Glasgow University Media Group, 1985, p 48-52.

Penguin Books for extracts from *Poverty in the United Kingdom: A survey of Household Resources and Standards of Living* © Peter Townsend, 1979, pp 19-24 and extracts from *The Health Divide* © Margaret Whitehead, 1988, pp 44-46.

The Policy Studies Institute for extracts from *Friendship Networks and Social Policy* by Peter Willmott, 1987, pp 25-28.

Shelter for extracts from *One Day I'll Have My Own Place to Stay*, p 92.

The Sun for 'Kids' Drug Orgy', p 100.

The University of London School Examinations Board for examination
  questions, pp 65, 114-115.

The University of Oxford Delegacy of Local Examinations for examination
  questions, p 65.

David Ward for 'When pupils are conned, not caned', p 72.

Celia Watson for 'Violence rare, teachers say', p 72.

The Women's Press Ltd. for extracts from *There's a Good Girl* by Marianne
  Grabrucker, 1989, p 80-81.

for permission to reproduce illustrations:

Shelter p 24
Mercury Press Agency Ltd p 56
Topham Picture Source p 59
The Controller of Her Majesty's Stationery Office p 101